Celebrate the Quilt

TWENTY QUILTS
FOR TWENTY YEARS

Compiled by Sally Schneider

Mission Statement

WE ARE DEDICATED TO PROVIDING QUALITY PRODUCTS AND SERVICES THAT INSPIRE CREATIVITY. WE WORK TOGETHER TO ENRICH THE LIVES WE TOUCH.

That Patchwork Place is a financially responsible ESOP company.

Celebrating the Quilt: Twenty Quilts for Twenty Years
© 1996 by That Patchwork Place, Inc.
PO Box 118, Bothell, WA 98041-0118 USA

Printed in Hong Kong
01 00 99 98 97   6 5 4 3 2

CREDITS

Editorial Director	Kerry I. Hoffman
Technical Editor	Sally Schneider
Managing Editor	Greg Sharp
Copy Editor	Liz McGehee
Proofreader	Melissa Riesland
Design Director	Judy Petry
Text and Cover Designer	Sandy Wing
Production Assistant	Shean Bemis
Illustrators	Laurel Strand
	Brian Metz
	Carolyn Kraft
Photographer	Brent Kane

Library of Congress Cataloging-in-Publication Data
Celebrating the quilt : twenty quilts for twenty years / compiled by Sally Schneider.
    p. cm.
    ISBN 1-56477-139-3
    1. Patchwork—patterns. 2. Quilting—patterns. 3. Appliqué—patterns.
4. Quilts. I. Schneider, Sally. II. That Patchwork Place, Inc.
TT835.C4 1996
746.46041—dc20   96-119
                            CIP

Table of Contents

Introduction

A quilt is a celebration of beauty, born from a vision of what can be, sculpted piece by piece with willing hands. It takes courage to believe in a vision when there are only a few hands and a great deal of work on the horizon. Nancy and Dan Martin have never been short on courage—or vision.

Somewhere in the fabric stash, bookcase, or sewing basket of millions of quilters throughout the world, there's almost surely a book with the familiar House on the Hill logo from the business Nancy and Dan started two decades ago: That Patchwork Place, home of "America's Best-Loved Quilt Books®."

Nancy had the passion to create, and Dan gave her the freedom to create without fear. "Don't ever worry about not having enough money to produce your ideas," he told her back then. "I'll take care of worrying about the money."

The House on the Hill logo has been around since the first kit Nancy put together in 1976 in the garage of her Oakland, New Jersey, home. Before the kit and the logo,

however, there was the beginning: the first time Nancy saw the magic of color, fabric, and design coming together in a new, yet old, way; the first time someone introduced her to quilting. Invited to work on a community quilt for the nation's bicentennial, she was hooked faster than you can say "patchwork."

It wasn't long before Nancy was incorporating simple patchwork projects into her craft classes. To make it easier for students, she assembled kits with coordinated fabrics, patterns, and instructions for simple designs like House on the Hill and Clay's Choice.

But this is not a patches-to-profits story of a home crafter with an idea who hit it big. Nancy is a skilled educator and an expert in preparing teaching materials. Her postgraduate studies focused on how people learn. Dan has a background in textile sales and business management. The pair wanted to be in business together. Their combined skills and knowledge were like a stack of fat quarters waiting for a quilter with an eye for color to pluck them from the shelf.

The first product Nancy developed was a patchwork kit for home crafters which included fabric and instructions to create a tie, purse flap, or pillow top. She assembled the kits and assumed Dan, the sales expert, would handle the rest, but he had other ideas. Selling would help her learn about the market and her future customers, he said. A big break came when *Seventeen* magazine saw her kit and asked for an interview. Soon she was filling mail orders and selling to retail outlets.

In 1977, Dan's work for Dupont took the couple west to Woodinville, a tree-studded suburb of Seattle, Washington. They converted a room over their garage into a studio where Nancy created a line of patterns and kits for vests, wall hangings, totes, and holiday decor. She sold the kits to area fabric stores and also offered them by mail order through national and regional sewing magazines.

One of her first retail outlets was a shop in Seattle, In the Beginning Fabrics. Now, eighteen years later, quilters from around the world can visit this popular store in a book written by owner Sharon Evans Yenter for That Patchwork Place's Quilt Shop Series.

When she wasn't creating and selling, Nancy was mingling with and learning from women who shared her passion for quilting. She joined Quilters Anonymous and met dozens of quilters at the monthly guild meetings. At each meeting, there were more new members. She listened as they voiced their concerns about the lack of good teaching materials.

That Patchwork Place outgrew Nancy's room-over-the-garage studio. She moved the business into a restored schoolhouse with a handful of employees, and there she taught classes, sold patterns and kits, and kept looking ahead. There were four dozen patterns and eleven instruction books in her line, but she knew the future was in books: quality full-color books that would teach, inspire, and foster innovation.

In 1981, Nancy asked Marsha McCloskey to write That Patchwork Place's first quilt book, *Small Quilts*. It was released nationally in 1982. More books followed: books written *by* quilters *for* quilters. That Patchwork Place authors are artists and teachers and, sometimes, risk takers, just like the woman whose creative spirit is still at the heart of the business.

"The quilting industry is like life," Nancy says. "The only thing that is constant is both growth and change."

Dan joined the company full time in January 1983, and That Patchwork Place has continued to evolve. Today the focus is books, with more than 150 in print.

Happy Endings—Finishing the Edges of Your Quilt by Mimi Dietrich has sold more than 200,000 copies, making it the company's best-selling book to date. Mimi was a quilting teacher who found that many of her students didn't know how to finish their quilts. That final step, she felt, is like the last scene of a good play—the rest isn't half as good without a stunning finish.

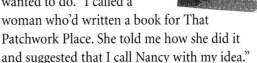

Mimi was also at a place in her life when she wanted to spend more time on her avocation—quilting—than her profession—teaching. She was reading a "What do you want to be when you grow up?" book, which recommended that she get in touch with someone who did what she wanted to do. "I called a woman who'd written a book for That Patchwork Place. She told me how she did it and suggested that I call Nancy with my idea."

That was 1986. More books from Mimi followed. Her most recent, *Quilts from the Smithsonian*, was a major challenge to her skills. You'll find one of Mimi's quilts in this book as well. "I had a lot of fun adapting one of my earlier designs and combining it with parts of some other favorite quilts to make something fresh and new," she says.

Celebrating the Quilt: Twenty Quilts for Twenty Years reflects the continuing goals for That Patchwork Place. It offers new challenges that experienced quilters seek and, at the same time, has a quilt or two for beginners. The Martins' goal is that each new book will be a trendsetter. "We don't want to be a publisher who's a 'me-too.' We want scoops; we want to be first and best," Nancy says.

Certainly the second-best all-time seller was that kind of scoop. *Watercolor Quilts* by Pat Maixner Magaret and Donna Ingram Slusser has quilters around the world using 2" squares like budding watercolor artists. The pair's third book, *Watercolor Impressions*, explores more variations on this theme.

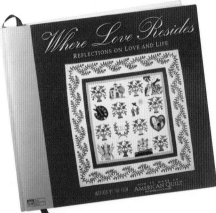

There was a lot of excitement at That Patchwork Place recently when the company was chosen by MCA/Universal/Amblin as the official licensee for a book based on the movie *How to Make an American Quilt. Where Love Resides*™ is an inspirational book based on the friendship blocks that were assembled into a wedding quilt in the film.

Hot-selling books equal company growth. Growth creates a space crunch. That's why That Patchwork Place has moved and ex-

panded several times over the years. Early in 1995, feeling slightly squeezed for space, the Martins asked their team of core leaders to find a building with 1,800 square feet of storage space to ease the pressure. The team came back with a two-story, 35,000-square-foot office building, which also had ample warehouse space. When you're an owner who supports risk and innovation, surprises are part of the package. The building had so much going for it that the Martins knew their core team's recommendation was right for the company's future.

In May 1995, That Patchwork Place moved to that building in Woodinville, now a showplace for the creativity that drives the company. There are quilts everywhere—from the foyer to individual work stations and the employees' lounge. This ever-changing quilt show is one reason why many folks sign up for tours that take place at 1 p.m. on Monday,

Wednesday, and Friday. Come along on one and you'll see quilts from the company's latest books as well as classics created in years past by Nancy and other employees.

The tour includes the second floor, where editors are working on books yet to be published. Here, fabric samples and quilt blocks are as common on desk tops as notepads. One editor has made a quilt from almost every book she's edited, so her work area will often have a design in progress pinned to the wall.

There's also a room where the newest quilting tools are tested. A sewing machine stands ready so an editor can check the author's instructions.

Downstairs, adjacent to the shipping and warehouse area, is a brand new photo studio with a 20-foot ceiling and state-of-the-art lighting. Here, quilts and garments are photographed for books. Photographs and illustrations are critical elements in any quilt book because quilters want to see the colors as they are in the original piece. Great care is given to ensure that the photo reproductions are accurate.

Many of the talented people who work at That Patchwork Place changed careers and are here because they love to quilt. If they are not quilters when they come, they usually develop an interest. Creativity is valued and respected in everyone, regardless of their job assignment. "We have always felt we should look for and hire skilled people who know more than we do about specific areas of the business," Dan says. "The growth we've had here comes from very talented people who are passionate about their work."

Dan is known as a motivator. "I tell (the staff) not to be afraid to step outside of their comfort zone." Support for innovation and risk taking is one of the reasons why each new book is unique.

That Patchwork Place also is a place where the ideas and opinions of customers are valued. Several employees spend their days answering phone calls on a toll-free line from

quilters around the country. Keeping in touch with the people who use the company's books and products is a must for Nancy, who teaches throughout the United States and abroad.

Once a year, quilters visit the company's home turf for a week-long frenzy of quilting and learning called "That Patchwork Place University." A woman from California sits next to a quilter from Australia and they exchange fat quarters and addresses. A Texan invites a Hong Kong quilter to dinner and the two women talk about quilts and family and everything in between. Friendships are made and renewed over sewing machines. Authors teach classes for all skill levels. Even beginners

can walk away with fresh confidence in their work. If there is something new in the quilting industry, you can bet That Patchwork Place University will have it.

At That Patchwork Place University, Nancy teaches and mingles and loves every minute of this time with quilters from around the world. She is there to learn from them, just as they have come to learn from her. Memories and snippets of inspiration are stored away for the quiet times in her studio. Quilting is, after all, an art of patience as well as passion.

Nancy sets aside at least two mornings a week for stitching, often in a beach-front cottage that is a family retreat. Her sewing companion most days is Cleo Nollette, a long-time friend whom she can count on for practical advice and straight talk, as well as straight stitching.

Nancy has a great stash of fabric in her studio, some of it gathered during her travels in Europe, Great Britain, Australia, and New Zealand. She stitches more than a dozen quilt tops a year and hand quilts smaller pieces

herself. Even if a piece is hand quilted for her, she always does the binding, that final step which makes a quilt truly her own.

From quiet times in the studio come new ideas for books and a vision. That vision blends into a melting pot of ideas from the people with whom she shares a future.

Recently, while quilts, stories, and patterns were moving into the hands of an editor who would shape it into this book, another "shaping" was taking place at That Patchwork Place. Dan, Nancy, and other company leaders set aside several days for a retreat to focus on the future of their publishing company. Out of that time of frank discussion and planning came some innovative ideas and a new mission statement:

"We are dedicated to providing quality products and services that inspire creativity. We work together to enrich the lives we touch."

Think of it as a promise to all who enjoy quilting and other needle arts. We're never going to be bored. There will always be something new to explore in this time-honored art form.

—*Linda Bryant*

Linda is a quilter and national award-winning newspaper columnist, who makes her home on Camano Island, Washington. In a box in her attic where Christmas decorations are stored, there is a quilted wall angel, stitched nearly twenty years ago from a That Patchwork Place pattern by Nancy Martin.

The staff of That Patchwork Place gathers in the lobby of their Woodinville, Washington, offices in celebration of the company's twentieth anniversary.

Projects

As quilters, we often mark anniversaries and other special occasions with quilts. To help That Patchwork Place celebrate its twentieth anniversary, each of its twenty top-selling authors was invited to make a special quilt. These quilts were purchased by That Patchwork Place and now form a part of its corporate collection. The authors were also asked to provide instructions so quilters all over the world could make their own special quilts. As an added treat, Nancy has related a short anecdote about each author; you will find these alongside the description of each quilt.

Each author was encouraged to design a project that was representative of her particular style or area of expertise. The only limit was the size of the quilt: it could not be larger than 280" around. There are no directions for basic quiltmaking techniques; these are readily available in any of our other books, some of which may already be on your shelf. Special techniques that apply to a specific quilt are included with the directions for that quilt.

See what's new from your favorite designer; celebrate with That Patchwork Place and our talented authors and make one, or *all*, of these very special quilts.

Easy Watercolor Baskets

SHARON EVANS YENTER

Sharon has owned In The Beginning Fabrics, a quilt shop in Seattle, Washington, for nineteen years. She is the author of the book, *In The Beginning*, part of That Patchwork Place's Quilt Shop Series.

Several years ago Northcott Silk, Inc., of Toronto, Canada, asked Sharon to make a quilt to display in their booth at Quilt Market. She was limited to using Northcott fabric, so out of necessity made a six-fabric watercolor quilt. Since that time, she has been designing a line of fabric for the company and enjoys making two- or three-fabric watercolor-style projects using her own floral designs and coordinates.

Designer's Statement   I would like to dedicate this quilt to Nancy Martin, president of That Patchwork Place, and her talented staff. They deserve baskets of flowers every day for the work they do to help and encourage quilters worldwide.

Easy Watercolor Baskets
Designed by Sharon Evans Yenter, 1994
Seattle, Washington
Finished Size: 38¾" x 51½"
Machine pieced and hand quilted by Margy Duncan

Materials: 44"-wide fabric

¼ yd. basket-weave print for baskets

½ yd. widely spaced light floral print for setting and corner triangles

1⅔ yds. off-white print or solid for Templates #1, #2, #3, and #6

½ yd. total assorted scraps to coordinate with florals for Template #1

½ yd. each of 3 contrasting florals, some of which include spaced, leafy areas with vines or tendrils, for Templates #1 and #5

1¼ yds. medium periwinkle print for inner border

46" x 60" piece of thin batting

1⅝ yds. for backing

½ yd. pink stripe for binding

Cutting

Use the patterns on page 122 to make templates for the pieces indicated below.

From the basket-weave print, cut:

6 large triangles (Template #4)

6 squares, each 2⅜" x 2⅜". Cut the squares once diagonally for 12 triangles (Template #5).

From the light floral print, cut:

2 squares, each 14" x 14". Cut the squares twice diagonally for setting triangles. You will have 2 extra triangles.

2 squares, each 6¾" x 6¾". Cut the squares once diagonally for 4 corner triangles.

From the off-white fabric, cut:

88 squares (Template #1); or cut 5 strips, each 2" x 42", then crosscut into 88 squares, each 2" x 2"

12 squares, each 3½" x 3½" (Template #2)

12 rectangles, each 2" x 6½" (Template #3)

6 triangles (Template #6) for the Basket blocks; or cut 3 squares, each 3⅞" x 3⅞", then cut each square once diagonally for 6 triangles (Note grain lines on the template.)

76 triangles (Template# 6) for the pieced border; or cut 19 squares, each 5½" x 5½", then cut each square twice diagonally for 76 triangles (Note grain lines on the template.)

From the assorted scraps, cut:

76 squares, each 2" x 2" (Template #1), for border

12 squares, each 2" x 2" (Template #1), for center block

From the contrasting floral and tendril fabrics*, cut:

114 squares (Template #1)

18 triangles (Template #5)

*Choose these pieces carefully so that multicolored florals are in the center of the block. Use some bright and some light to medium flowers. Use the leaves and tendrils around the outer edges of the block. The fabric will resemble Swiss cheese when you are finished because of your selective cutting.

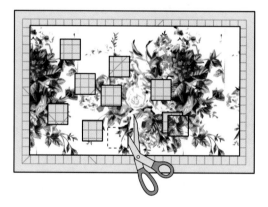

From the medium periwinkle print, cut:

2 strips, each 2⅝" x 45", cut on the lengthwise grain, for inner border

2 strips, each 2⅝" x 32", cut on the lengthwise grain, for inner border

Block Construction

1. Arrange Template #1 squares of off-white and assorted scrap fabrics as shown below. Sew the squares together to make 6 four-patch units.

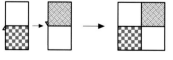

Make 6.

2. Arrange four-patch units and off-white Template #2 squares as shown below. Sew the squares together in rows; press the seams in the direction shown. Sew the rows together to make 2 center blocks.

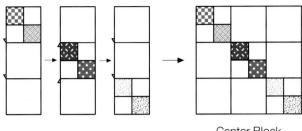

Center Block
Make 2.

3. Arrange 19 Template #1 squares and 3 Template #5 triangles to form the bouquet as shown below, carefully arranging the floral and tendril fabrics to look like a bouquet of flowers. All the outer squares should be tendril or leaf fabric. Work with the bouquet until you are satisfied with the placement of the flowers and leaves.

4. Sew the squares and triangles together in vertical rows as shown; press seams in opposite directions from row to row. Make 6 bouquet units. Add a basket-weave triangle (Template #4) to the base of each bouquet to form the basket. Press the seam toward the triangle.

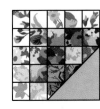

Make 6.

5. Arrange the off-white rectangles (Template #3), basket triangles (Template #5), and off-white triangles (Template #6) and sew them together as shown to complete the Basket blocks. Make 6 blocks.

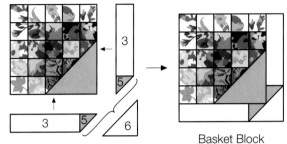

Basket Block
Make 6.

Quilt Top Assembly and Finishing

1. Arrange all the blocks with the setting triangles as shown. Sew the blocks and triangles together in diagonal rows, pressing seams in opposite directions from row to row. Be careful not to stretch the bias edges of the setting triangles when joining them to the blocks. Sew the diagonal rows together. Add the 4 corner triangles last.

2. Arrange the remaining background and colored squares to make 38 Four Patch blocks and sew them together as shown in step 1 of "Block Construction" on page 12.

3. Sew an off-white triangle (Template #6) to each side of 34 of the four-patch units as shown to make side units for the pieced border. Press the seams toward the block.

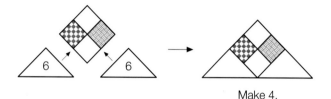

Make 34.

4. Arrange the remaining four-patch units and triangles as shown below and sew them together to make 4 corner units.

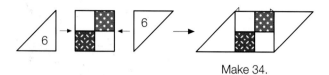

Make 4.

5. Join side and corner units to make borders as shown below. Make 2 border strips with 10 side units and 1 corner unit. Make 2 border strips with 7 side units and 1 corner unit.

Top and Bottom Borders
Make 2.

Side Borders
Make 2.

6. Sew 1 periwinkle print border strip to the shorter side of each pieced border strip as shown.

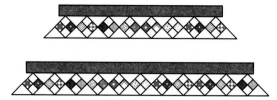

7. Sew the borders to the quilt top, mitering the corners.
8. Layer the quilt top with backing and batting; baste. Quilt as desired or follow the quilting suggestion below. Quilt diagonal lines except around the flowers in the baskets. Follow the outlines of the floral fabric and tendrils to accentuate the curves in the bouquets.

9. Add a hanging sleeve and a label to the back of the quilt. Bind the edges with 2½"-wide, double-fold bias strips of pink striped fabric.

Spinning Stars

TRUDIE HUGHES

Trudie lives in Elm Grove, Wisconsin, where her quilt shop of twenty years, Patched Works, is also located. She is a pioneer in developing quilts that are cut without templates. Trudie has written eleven books, including *Template-Free® Quiltmaking, More Template-Free® Quiltmaking, Even More,* and *Template-Free® Quilts and Borders,* and designed three rulers to use with the rotary cutter. She teaches and lectures nationally and has traveled widely.

Designer's Statement This quilt is representative of the cutting techniques that I use to make my quilts. This one uses the "Speedy" feature on my Rotary Mate™ ruler. Ever since I wrote my first book, I have been interested in Snowball blocks and love to use them in my quilt designs. This quilt, designed for the celebration of That Patchwork Place's twentieth anniversary, features this old-favorite Spinning Star block, set off in frames and surrounded with an interesting pieced border.

Spinning Stars
by Trudie Hughes, 1995
Elm Grove, Wisconsin
Finished Size: 48" x 48"

Materials: 44"-wide fabric

2 yds. background for blocks and borders
2½ yds. total assorted bright red, yellow, blue, green, orange, and purple prints for blocks, borders, and binding
56" x 56" piece of batting
3 yds. for backing

Cutting

From the background fabric, cut:

5 strips, each 2⅝" x 42". Open all strips and layer them right sides up; crosscut into 36 rectangles, each 2⅝" by 4⅞". Align the 45° line of the Rotary Mate on the bottom of the rectangle so that the right edge of the ruler intersects the corner. Cut along the edge of the ruler. Discard the triangles or set them aside for another project.

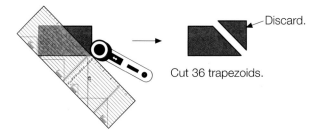

Cut 36 trapezoids.

5 strips, each 1⅝" x 42". Open all strips and layer them right sides up; crosscut 36 rectangles, each 1⅝" x 5". Align the 45° line of the Rotary Mate on the top of the rectangle so that the right edge of the ruler intersects the corner. Cut along the edge of the ruler.

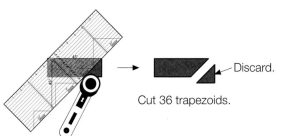

Cut 36 trapezoids.

2 strips, each 6½" x 42". Crosscut 9 squares, each 6½" x 6½". Using the 2" Speedy* on the Rotary Mate, remove all 4 corners to create 9 snowballs.

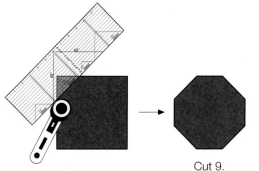

Cut 9.

*If you do not have the Rotary Mate, trace the triangle pattern (page 129) on plain white paper and cut it out. Tape the triangle to the bottom of your ruler as shown and use this to remove the corners from the squares.

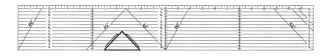

8 strips, each 1½" x 42". From 4 strips, crosscut 12 rectangles, each 1½" x 12½", for sashing strips. From 2 strips, cut 2 pieces, each 1½" x 38½", for top and bottom inner borders. From 2 strips, cut 2 pieces, each 1½" x 40½", for side inner borders.

Reserve the remaining background fabric for the pieced border.

From the assorted bright prints:

Cut a total of 18 assorted squares, each 5½" x 5½"; cut twice diagonally for 72 assorted quarter-square triangles.

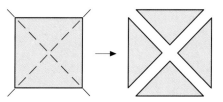

From each of 9 different prints, cut 2 strips, each 1⅜" x 42". From each fabric, cut 2 strips, each 1⅜" x 10¾", and 2 strips, each 1⅜" x 12½", for the block borders.

From each of 4 different prints, cut 1 square, 1½" x 1½", for the cornerstones. Set the remaining fabric aside for the pieced border.

Block Construction

1. Sew each of the large trapezoids to a bright-colored quarter-square triangle to make Unit A. Offset the edges of the triangle as shown. *Stitch carefully; you are sewing a bias seam.* Press the seam toward the triangle.

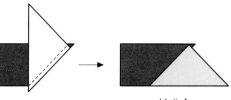

Unit A
Make 36.

2. Sew each of the smaller trapezoids to the side of one of the remaining triangles to make Unit B. Press the seams toward the trapezoid.

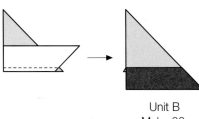

Unit B
Make 36.

3. Sew a Unit A to the longer (bias) edge of a Snowball block. Sew the seam approximately halfway and stop. Finger-press the seam toward the triangle.

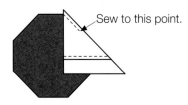

Sew to this point.

4. Add a Unit B, aligning the right edge of the trapezoid with the triangle and offsetting the points on the left edge by ¼". Press all seams toward the triangles.

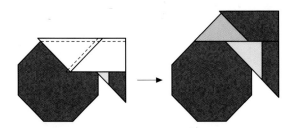

5. Alternate adding Unit A and B, using a variety of bright colors in each block. Stitch the remaining sections of the first seam. The blocks should measure 10¾" from raw edge to raw edge.

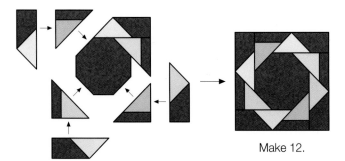

Make 12.

6. Sew a 1⅜" x 10¾" strip to opposite side edges of the quilt block; press the seams toward the strips. Sew 1⅜" x 12½" strips to the top and bottom edges of the block. Press.

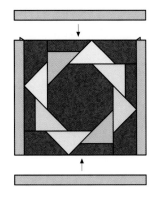

Quilt Top Assembly and Finishing

1. Arrange the blocks with the 4 cornerstones and sashing strips. Sew them together in rows, alternating blocks and sashing strips. Sew sashing strips and cornerstones together in rows. Press seams toward the sashing strips. Sew the rows together.

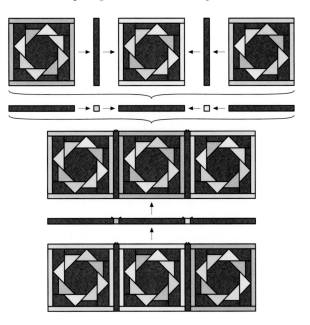

2. Sew the 1½" x 38½" strips to the top and bottom edges of the quilt top. Press the seams toward the border strips. Sew the 1½" x 40" strips to the side edges of the quilt top.

3. Cut the following for the pieced border.
   From the background fabric, cut:
   > 2 strips, each 5¼" x 42". Crosscut 10 squares, each 5¼" x 5¼". Cut the squares twice diagonally for 40 quarter-square triangles.
   >
   > 4 squares, each 4½" x 4½", for corners

   From the assorted bright-colored prints, cut:
   > 10 assorted squares, each 5¼" x 5¼". Cut the squares twice diagonally for 40 quarter-square triangles.
   >
   > 20 assorted squares, each 4⅞" x 4⅞". Cut the squares once diagonally for 40 half-square triangles.

4. Place each of 20 bright-colored quarter-square triangles right sides together with a triangle of background fabric. Chain-piece 20 pairs with the print on top as shown. Press the seams toward the darker fabric.

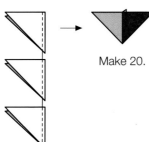

Make 20.

5. Chain-piece the remaining 20 pairs with the background on top as shown. Press seams toward the darker fabric.

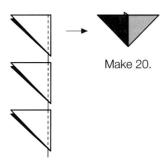

Make 20.

6. Sew each pieced triangle to a half-square triangle of bright-colored print. Press the seam toward the larger triangle in each square.

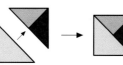

Make 20.

Make 20.

7. Arrange the units as shown to make 4 identical border strips, noting the placement of the background fabric and the large triangle. Add a black square to each end of 2 border strips.

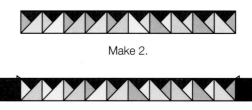

Make 2.

Make 2.

8. Sew the shorter border strips to opposite side edges of the quilt top. Press the seams toward the inner border. Sew the remaining border strips to the top and bottom edges of the quilt top.

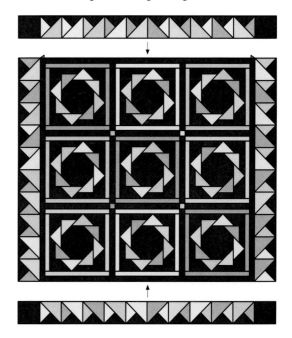

9. Layer the quilt top with backing and batting; baste. Quilt as desired or quilt ¼" from each seam throughout the quilt.

10. Add a hanging sleeve and a label to the back of the quilt. Cut 1¾"-wide straight-grain binding strips from the leftover bright-colored prints. Trim them to varying lengths and sew them together with a diagonal seam to make 1 piece of binding that is long enough for your quilt. Bind the edges of the quilt.

Marsha is a longtime friend, whose accurate piecing techniques and design style have influenced my work tremendously. Marsha wrote the first quilting book, Small Quilts, for That Patchwork Place. Her first books were responsible for the early success of That Patchwork Place. Marsha and I co-authored several books, including A Dozen Variables and Ocean Waves. She now heads her own business, Feathered Star Productions, which produces quality quilting books and markets the work of others. Her new fabric line, Staples, is delighting quilters everywhere as they revel in a wide range of choices for background fabrics.

—NJM

Stairway to Heaven

MARSHA MCCLOSKEY

Marsha has been quilting since 1969 and is well known throughout the quilting world. A graphic arts major in college, Marsha turned from printmaking to quiltmaking as motherhood made the messier media impractical. The weekly Saturday Market in Eugene, Oregon, provided a handy outlet for her earliest efforts. She found that the more quilts and small items she sold, the more she had to make to replace them. Such daily practice increased her skills as a seamstress and fabric artist. This also marked the beginning of many years of producing patchwork gift items for craft fairs and gift shops in the Pacific Northwest and California.

Marsha started teaching quiltmaking in 1975 and has taught classes and workshops in the Seattle area where she lives, as well as for conferences and quilt guilds in thirty-eight states. She has also taught internationally, traveling to Australia, Holland, Belgium, France, Canada, Japan, Norway, and Denmark.

She wrote That Patchwork Place's first quilting book, *Small Quilts. Wall Quilts* followed quickly on its heels. She has since written many other books, including *On to Square Two, Projects for Blocks and Borders, Christmas Quilts, Feathered Star Quilts, Stars and Stepping Stones, Lessons in Machine Piecing,* and *Feathered Star Sampler.* With Nancy Martin, she co-authored *A Dozen Variables* and *Ocean Waves.*

Marsha continues to make and design quilts, write quilt books, travel, and teach. She has her own small publishing company, Feathered Star Productions, and in 1995 she designed a line of quilting fabrics, Staples, for the Clothworks label.

Designer's Statement   I made "Stairway to Heaven" in 1989 for my book *Stars and Stepping Stones.* Of all the quilts I made for the book, it was my favorite, but as often happens in publishing, we ran out of available pages and the pattern was cut from the book. I was disappointed because I liked the quilt, and it was one of the first where I experimented with yellow. When I was invited to contribute to this anniversary book, I was pleased to finally have a place to showcase the quilt.

The block is a versatile design and a wonderful piecing challenge. Normally, I don't make blocks with so many set-in seams, but this LeMoyne Star is circled with squares (stepping-stones) and I just couldn't resist. As I stitched on my blocks, I felt that sense of accomplishment and satisfaction that comes with tackling a difficult task and doing it well. It was really fun!

Stairway to Heaven
by Marsha McCloskey, 1989
Seattle, Washington
Finished Size: 49" x 49"
Quilted by Freda Smith.

Materials: 44"-wide fabric

¼ yd. light green print for blocks

½ yd. total assorted yellow prints for blocks and pieced border

2 yds. total assorted lavender and purple prints for blocks, pieced border, and outer border

¾ yd. periwinkle print for lattices and pieced border

54" x 54" piece of batting

3 yds. for backing

¾ yd. for binding

Cutting

Each block has a different arrangement of values and colors. Study the color photo on page 21 for color placement or create your own color and value variations.

Make templates using the patterns on pages 123–24.

From the assorted light green, yellow, and lavender prints, cut:

128 total assorted squares, each 2" x 2" (Template #1)

9 squares, each 2½" x 2½" (Template #5), for setting squares

From the assorted lavender prints, cut 32 trapezoids (Template #2) and 32 trapezoids (Template #3).

From the assorted lavender and yellow prints, cut 32 diamonds (Template #4). To rotary cut these pieces, cut 2⅝"-wide strips. Make a 45° diagonal cut at one end of the strip. Make additional cuts parallel to the first 45° diagonal cut, measuring 2⅝" each time.

Cutting Diamonds

From the periwinkle print, cut 12 lattice strips, each 2½" x 15".

Block Construction

1. Referring to the color photo on page 21, arrange 4 squares, each 2" x 2" (Template #1), for each four-patch unit. Sew and press as shown. Make a total of 32 units, 8 for each block.

Four-Patch Unit
Make 32.

2. Sew each large trapezoid (Template #3) to a small trapezoid (Template #2). Press seam toward large trapezoid. Make a total of 32 units, 8 for each block.

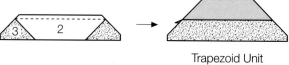

Trapezoid Unit
Make 32.

3. Join a four-patch unit to 2 diamonds (Template #4) as shown; sew with the four-patch unit on top. Begin and end stitching at the ¼" seam line. Press the seams toward the diamonds. Make 16 diamond units, 4 for each block.

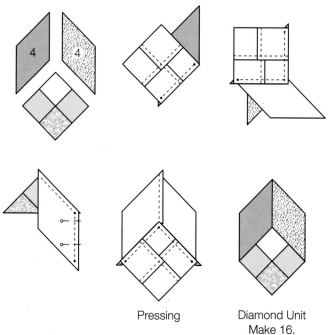

Pressing   Diamond Unit
                  Make 16.

Tip: Lightly mark the stitching start and stop positions on the wrong side of each four-patch unit. Be as precise as possible. Use pins to accurately position the intersections of the stitching lines at the star points and to pin interfering seam allowances out of the way. Press seams toward the darker fabric or the way they want to go.

4. Join 1 four-patch unit to 2 trapezoids as shown. Press the seams toward the four-patch unit. Make 16 corner units, 4 for each block.

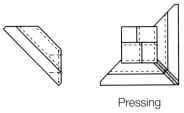

5. Sew the trapezoids together and press the seam open.

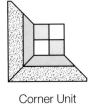

Pressing   Corner Unit

6. Join each corner unit to a diamond unit as shown. Make 16 units, 4 for each block. Press the seams as shown.

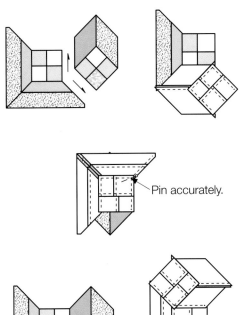

Pin accurately.

Pressing

7. Join the completed units as shown below to make half blocks. Sew the seams in the order indicated. Make 8 half blocks, 2 for each block.

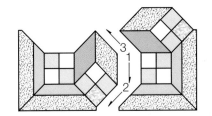

Sew seams in numerical order.

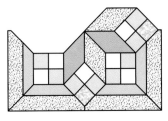

Half Blocks
Make 2 for each block.

8. To complete the blocks, join the half blocks. Pin the intersections of the star points and the star center; sew carefully. Sew the seams in the order indicated. Make 4 blocks.

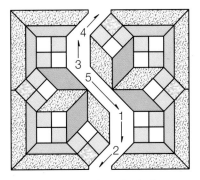

Sew seams in order in the direction of the arrows.

Quilt Top Assembly and Finishing

1. Arrange the blocks, lattice strips, and setting squares as shown. Sew the blocks and sashing strips together in rows, pressing the seams toward the sashing. Sew sashing strips and setting squares together to make 3 rows. Press all seams toward the sashing strips. Sew the rows together.

2. Measure the quilt top for straight-cut borders. From a dark purple print, cut 4 strips, each 1" x 36". Trim 2 strips to fit the sides; sew them to the side edges of the quilt top. Trim the 2 remaining strips to fit the top and bottom; sew to the top and bottom edges of the quilt top. Press the seams toward the borders.

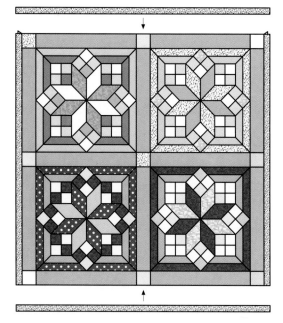

Note: If your seam allowances are larger or smaller than ¼" wide, resulting in a quilt that is larger or smaller than indicated in the directions, you may adjust the width of this border to make the Chain of Squares pieced border fit better. Wait to cut it until you have constructed the pieced border sections, then measure the quilt center (blocks sewn with lattices) and the top and bottom border strips (the ones that end with a Template #7 triangle). Subtract the quilt center measurement from the pieced border measurement. Divide the answer by 2, then add ½" for seam allowances. Cut your border strips this width.

3. Cut the following pieces for the Chain of Squares border:

   From the assorted yellow prints, cut:

   14 squares, each 4¹⁄₁₆" x 4¹⁄₁₆". Cut the squares twice diagonally for 56 triangles (Template #6).

   2 squares, each 2⁵⁄₁₆" x 2⁵⁄₁₆". Cut the squares once diagonally for 4 triangles (Template #7).

   From the assorted lavender prints, cut:

   56 squares, each 2½" x 2½" (Template #5)

   From the periwinkle print, cut:

   13 squares, each 4¹⁄₁₆" x 4¹⁄₁₆". Cut the squares twice diagonally for 52 triangles (Template #6).

   2 squares, each 2⁵⁄₁₆" x 2⁵⁄₁₆". Cut the squares once diagonally for 4 triangles (Template #7).

4. Referring to the color photograph on page 21 and the illustrations below, assemble 2 side border sections and 2 top and bottom border sections. Assemble 4 corner sections.

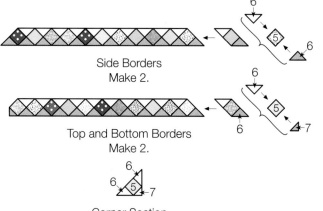

Side Borders
Make 2.

Top and Bottom Borders
Make 2.

Corner Section
Make 4.

5. Add the borders to the quilt top; add the top and bottom borders first, then add the side borders. Add the corner sections last.

Add corner sections last.

6. For the outer border, cut 4 lavender strips, each 4¼" x 42". From another lavender, cut 4 squares, each 4¼" x 4¼" (Template #8), for corner squares.

7. Measure the quilt top for all 4 border strips as shown below. Trim 4 border strips to fit the quilt top. Sew 2 strips to the side edges of the quilt top.

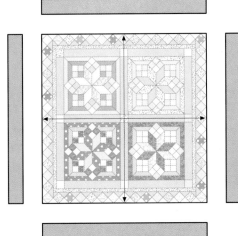

Measure and cut 2 side borders and a top and bottom border.

8. Sew 1 square to each end of the 2 remaining border strips. Press the seams toward the border. Sew the strips to the top and bottom edges of the quilt top.

9. Layer the quilt top with backing and batting; baste. Quilt as desired or follow the quilting suggestion below. Quilt in-the-ditch on the blocks and the pieced border, and elongated hexagons in the lattice strips. Quilt a double cable on the outer border.

10. Add a hanging sleeve and a label to the back of the quilt. Bind the edges of the quilt with 1½"-wide, single-layer strips of bias binding.

We often refer to generous or gifted people as having a "heart of gold." Here is how Nancy's "heart" got her out of a jam.

On a 1989 teaching trip to New Zealand, several teachers and their hosts went to a Chinese restaurant. During the evening, Nancy left for the restroom. When she was ready to go back to the table, she discovered that her stall had latched from the outside. The door extended all the way to the floor and almost to the ceiling. She was trapped. She waited patiently for someone to come and let her out, but nobody came.

Realizing that she would have to find her own way out, she looked at her necklace with its big gold heart and saw that the edge could substitute as a screwdriver. Using the heart, the ever-resourceful Nancy unscrewed the door from its hinges. When she returned to the table an hour later, she discovered the others had been laughing so hard they hadn't even missed her!

—Mary Hickey

Anniversary Rose

NANCY J. MARTIN

Nancy is a talented author, teacher, and quiltmaker, who has written more than twenty-six books on quiltmaking. The ever-popular *Pieces of the Past* and *Threads of Time* explore quilting history. Nancy and Marsha McCloskey collaborated on several books that introduced rotary cutting, multi-fabric quilts, and the Bias Square® cutting guide to quilters everywhere. Their books, *Back to Square One, A Dozen Variables,* and *Ocean Waves,* have become standards in quilting libraries. Nancy wrote *Rotary Riot* and *Rotary Roundup,* two recent best sellers on quick cutting, with co-author Judy Hopkins. Her *Fun with Fat Quarters* incorporates more than eighteen years of teaching experience into helpful information for beginning quilters. *Simply Scrappy Quilts,* Nancy's latest book, focuses on her love of scrap quilts.

Nancy, president of That Patchwork Place, Inc., is an avid quiltmaker and loves to display her work throughout her home. She has written two books that focus on quilts as part of interior design, *Make Room for Quilts* and *At Home with Quilts.*

Designer's Statement   Although encouraged to design a quilt that was representative of my style or area of expertise, I had just completed *Simply Scrappy Quilts* and couldn't force myself to make one more bias square! So I decided on a pieced quilt embellished with appliqué as a change of pace. The large-scale chintz and scrappy assortment of fabrics are typical elements in many of my quilts. I first chose the Waverly® print for the center of the blocks, then chose an assortment of burgundy and green fabrics to coordinate with it. To soften the angular lines of the block, I appliquéd small pomegranate (or love apple) designs over the corners of the block. Narrow sashing that matches the background fabric helps create a pleasing pattern where the appliqué pomegranates meet.

Anniversary Rose
by Nancy J. Martin, 1995
Woodinville, Washington
Finished Size: 72" x 72"
Quilted by Alvina Nelson.

Materials: 44"-wide fabric

2¼ yds. large-scale print for block centers and outer border

1½ yds. total assorted burgundy prints for blocks and appliqué*

¾ yd. total assorted dark green prints for blocks**

1⅝ yds. light background print for block corners and sashing

½ yd. burgundy print for inner border

¾ yd. green solid for appliqué

⅜ yd. rose solid for appliqué

¼ yd. yellow solid for appliqué

78" x 78" piece of batting

4⅜ yds. for backing

½ yd. green print for bias binding

*Substitute 6 fat quarters if desired.
**Substitute 4 fat quarters if desired.

Cutting

Using the appliqué patterns on page 124, make templates and cut the pieces from appropriate fabrics.

From the large-scale print, cut:

2 strips, each 7¾" x 58½", from the *lengthwise grain* for outer side borders

2 strips, each 7¾" x 73½", from the *lengthwise grain* for outer top and bottom borders

9 squares, each 4½" x 4½", for block centers

From the burgundy prints, cut:

3 strips, each 6⅞" x 42". Crosscut 18 squares, each 6⅞" x 6⅞". Cut the squares once diagonally for 36 triangles.

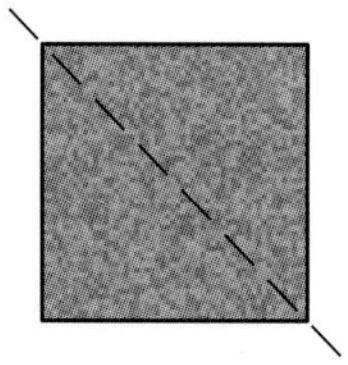

4 strips, each 5¼" x 42". Crosscut 27 squares, each 5¼" x 5¼". Cut the squares twice diagonally for 108 triangles.

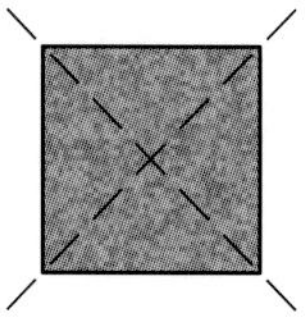

From the dark green prints, cut:

8 strips, each 2⅞" x 42". Crosscut 108 squares, each 2⅞" x 2⅞". Cut the squares once diagonally for 216 triangles.

From the light background print, cut:

3 strips, each 6⅞" x 42". Crosscut 18 squares, each 6⅞" x 6⅞". Cut the squares once diagonally for 36 triangles.

3 strips, each 2½" x 42". Crosscut 6 rectangles, each 2½" x 16½", for sashing.

9 strips, each 2½" x 42", for sashing. Cut 3 strips in half crosswise and sew 1 short strip to each of the 6 remaining strips. Trim them to make 4 strips, each 2½" x 52½", and 2 strips, each 2½" x 56½", for sashing.

From the burgundy print for the inner border, cut:

36 of Template #3 (flower)

6 strips, each 1½" x 42". Cut 2 strips in half crosswise and sew 1 piece to each of the 4 remaining strips. Trim them to make 2 strips, each 1½" x 56½", and 2 strips, each 1½" x 58½", for inner borders.

From the green solid, cut:

36 of Template #2 (flower base)

72 of Template #6 (small leaf)

36 of Template #1 (stem)

72 of Template #7 (large leaf)

From the rose solid, cut:

36 of Template #4 (flower)

From the yellow solid, cut:

36 of Template #5 (flower)

Block Construction

1. Join each large triangle of light background print to a large burgundy print triangle. Press the seam toward the burgundy fabric. Fold the unit in half diagonally, opposite the seam line, and crease to make an appliqué placement line.

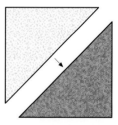

Make 36.

2. Appliqué the flower, stem, and leaves on each piece. Refer to the illustration at right for placement.

Make 36.

3. Sew 1 dark green print triangle to each side of a small burgundy print triangle to make flying-geese units. Repeat to make 108 units, 12 for each block.

Make 108.

4. Sew the units together in rows of 3 units each.

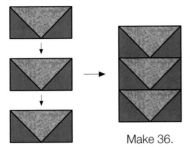

Make 36.

5. Arrange the flying-geese units, appliqué squares, and center squares as shown below; sew them together to make 9 blocks. Press the seams as shown below.

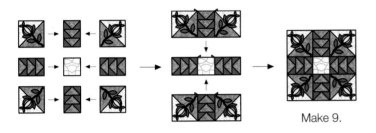

Make 9.

Quilt Top Assembly and Finishing

1. Join 3 blocks and 2 sashing strips, each 2½" x 16½", to make a row. Make 3 rows.

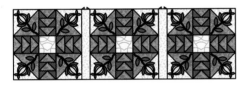

Make 3.

2. Arrange the 3 rows of blocks and 4 strips of sashing, each 2½" x 52½", as shown below; sew them together. Sew the 2½" x 56½" sashing strips to the top and bottom edges to complete the quilt top. Press all seams toward the sashing strips.

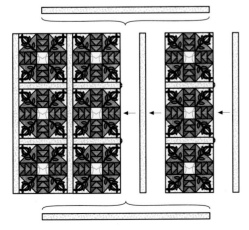

3. Measure the quilt top for straight-cut borders. Trim 2 strips of burgundy border fabric to fit the sides; sew them to the side edges of the quilt top. Press all seams toward the burgundy border. Measure and trim the remaining 2 burgundy border strips to fit the top and bottom; sew them to the top and bottom edges of the quilt top.

4. Add the outer borders in the same manner.

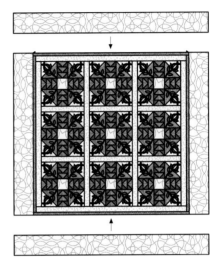

5. Layer the quilt top with batting and backing; baste. Quilt as desired or follow the quilting suggestion below. Quilt in-the-ditch around the triangles and appliqué motifs. Use a 1" crosshatch pattern in the light background fabrics behind the appliqué. Quilt a narrow feather quilting design in the sashing and a larger rope design in the border.

6. Add a hanging sleeve and a label to the back of the quilt. Bind the edges of the quilt with 2½"-wide, double-fold bias strips.

Matisse's Garden Baskets

MARY HICKEY

While working on her twentieth-anniversary quilt, Mary realized with dismay that she was now an old-timer with That Patchwork Place. Mary began her love affair with quilts in college color and design classes. She began her association with That Patchwork Place in the 1980s when she started work on her first book, *Little by Little*. Mary is a prolific designer, author, quiltmaker, and popular international teacher. Her books include *Angle Antics, Basket Garden, Pioneer Storybook Quilts*, and *A Pioneer Doll and Her Quilts*. With Nancy Martin, Sara Nephew, and Marsha McCloskey, she is a co-author of *Quick & Easy Quiltmaking*, and with Joan Hanson, she wrote *The Joy of Quilting*.

Mary's continuous search for easier and more accurate ways of piecing led her to design the BiRangle™ ruler for making the long, thin triangles that create the tulip petals in this quilt. In addition to quilting, Mary loves baseball, opera, and bird watching. However, it is her love of gardening that inspired "Matisse's Garden Baskets."

Mary remembers with pride that she learned the value of duct tape while setting up picket fences, spotlights, and book displays for That Patchwork Place's booth at early quilt trade shows. She recalls with chagrin the day she stapled the marketing vice-president's jacket sleeve to the top of a display table. Unfortunately, the sleeve was still on the vice-president's arm. Most of all, she recognizes with great gratitude That Patchwork Place's role in providing an incredible opportunity for a career and an outlet for her creativity.

Designer's Statement   A meadow of lush green surrounds these cheerful baskets of tulips. The vivid tulip shapes dance in a predictable pattern, giving the quilt a slight sense of order, while the sweeping leaves and stems and the randomly placed colors create a whirl of joyous energy. Consider making the twenty pieced tulips in the center section of the quilt for your own special twentieth anniversary. Then add the outer border of tulips to symbolize the power and effect of your own creativity on those around you.

Mary is a truly delightful person to be around—just ask anyone who has seen her Mrs. Buff Orpington skit. Trained as an artist, Mary has a discerning eye, which is evident in her quilt designs, the decorative painting she has added to her home, and the charming little cottage she and her husband, Phil, recently renovated. Mary's hobbies include raising chickens. After working on Quick & Easy Quiltmaking, *she named three new chicks after her co-authors. There was a chicken named Sara, one named Marsha (who was subsequently eaten by the neighbor's dog), and a Polish hen named Nancy because it reminded Mary of my wild hairdo.*

—NJM

Matisse's Garden Baskets
by Mary Hickey, 1995
Keyport, Washington
Finished Size: 46½" x 46½"

Materials: 44"-wide fabric:

Note: Mary used one shade of green for the center section of the quilt and a slightly darker green for the border. She suggests that you purchase enough of one green fabric to make the entire quilt. (That's what she meant to do!)

2½ yds. light green print for background

⅜ yd. assorted red prints for tulips

⅜ yd. assorted blue prints for tulips

¼ yd. assorted yellow prints for tulips

¼ yd. assorted white prints for tulips

¼ yd. assorted pink prints for tulips

¼ yd. pink print for tulip centers and four-patch units

¼ yd. pale blue print for tulip centers and four-patch units

¼ yd. pale yellow print for tulip centers and four-patch units

¼ yd. pale pink print for tulip centers and four-patch units

⅓ yd. basket-weave print for baskets

⅝ yd. dark green print for appliqué and pieced leaves

¼ yd. medium green print for stems

¾ yd. medium green print for inner and outer borders

54" x 54" piece of batting

2 yds. fabric for backing

⅝ yd. fabric for binding

Making the Bias Rectangles

When 2 long, thin triangles are sewn together, the resulting shape is a rectangle. By using a BiRangle ruler, you can make many rectangles (half-rectangle units) quickly and easily!

1. **From the red and the dark green for leaves, cut** 2 strips, each 4½" x 42", for a total of 4 strips. **From each of the remaining tulip fabrics, cut** 1 strip, 4½" x 42". **From the light green background, cut** 8 strips, each 4½" x 42".

2. Layer 1 strip of green background and 1 strip of tulip color, *both right side down,* on your cutting mat. Fold the fabrics in half and place the fold on the right.

4½"-wide strips ⟶   ⟵ Fold

3. Place the diagonal line of your BiRangle on the right edge of the fabrics. Push a long ruler next to the BiRangle, remove the BiRangle, and cut along the right edge of the long ruler.

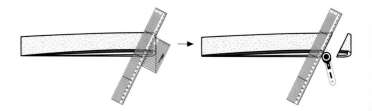

4. Turn your mat around and cut the layers into 2½"-wide bias strips; make cuts parallel to the first cut.

5. Sort the strips into 2 sets, up-facing ones and down-facing ones. These strips are sneaky and love to confuse you, so place the up-facing set in the kitchen for now.

6. Sew the down-facing set of strips into 2 strip sets, each containing 7 strips, alternating the colors. Offset the tops of the strips ¼" as shown, since it will save you a great deal of fabric. When they are sewn into a unit, the tops of the strips form a relatively straight line. Press the seams toward the darker color.

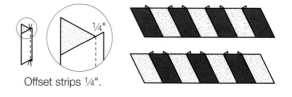

Offset strips ¼".

7. Place one sewn strip set on your mat. Place the BiRangle on the strip set with the diagonal line on one of the center seam lines, and the short side parallel to the top edge of the unit. Align your long cutting ruler with the edge of the BiRangle. Slide both toward the top edge until the ruler is on the least amount of fabric possible. Remove the BiRangle.

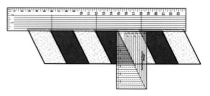

8. Trim the edge. Only a few threads will need to be trimmed at one end, while as much as 1" or more will have to be trimmed from the other end. Each time

you make this trimming cut, you are actually cutting one side of many rectangles, so you can see how important it is to line up the two rulers and trim.

9. Cut a 3½"-wide segment. As you cut this segment, you are cutting the second side of each rectangle.

→ Trim

→ Segment

→ Excess

10. To cut the rectangles, place the edge of the BiRangle on the edge of the fabric, with the diagonal line on the seam line. If you are right-handed, line everything up on the right and cut on the right. As you cut, you are cutting the third side of each rectangle. If you are left-handed, turn these pages upside down and follow the diagrams.

11. Move the BiRangle to the next seam line. Make sure the edge of the BiRangle is on the edge of the fabric. Cut on the right side of every seam line. Continue this process until you have cut the entire segment.

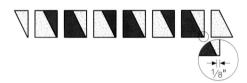

1/8"

12. Turn your mat around so all your right-hand cuts are moved to the left. Reposition your BiRangle so the diagonal line is on the seam line and the edge of the BiRangle is on the edge of the fabric; trim.

1/8"

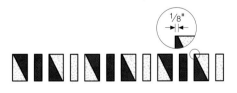

The rectangles will be 2" x 3½". The seam should *not* come through the corner of the rectangle, but should be about ⅛" from the corner.

13. Sew the second set of strips together and repeat the steps above to make a second set of rectangles. *To cut the second segments and rectangles, you must turn the strip set over and cut from the back of the fabrics.* Press the seams of this unit toward the lighter color.

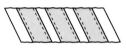

14. Repeat steps 2–13 above, pairing each remaining background strip with a strip of dark green (for leaves) or tulip fabric. You will need the following total *pairs* of bias rectangles: 16 red, 12 blue, 8 yellow, 8 white, 4 pink, and 20 dark green.

Cutting

From the light green background print, cut:
   10 strips, each 2" x 42". From 2 of the strips, cut 8 rectangles, each 2" x 9½" for the Basket blocks. From 2 of the strips, cut 20 rectangles, each 2" x 3½", for the Tulip blocks. From the remaining 6 strips, cut 116 squares, each 2" x 2", for the Tulip blocks.
   4 squares, each 11" x 11"
   2 squares, each 3⅞" x 3⅞". Cut the squares once diagonally for 4 triangles.
From the assorted prints for tulips, cut a total of 48 squares, each 2" x 2".
From the prints for tulip centers and four-patch units, cut a total of 76 squares, each 2" x 2".
From the basket-weave print, cut:
   4 squares, each 6½" x 6½". You may prefer to cut the squares on the bias to have the fabric design appear in a pleasing direction. If so, take great care when handling the squares to avoid stretching the bias edges.
   4 squares, each 2⅜" x 2⅜"; cut each square once diagonally for 8 triangles

Block Construction

1. Sew 20 tulip 2" squares to 20 light green 2" squares. Press the seams toward the darker square. Sew a 2" x 3½" rectangle of light green to each unit to make tulip centers. Press the seams toward the rectangle.

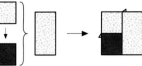

Make 20.

2. Make 20 Tulip blocks, using the half-rectangle units, tulip-center units, and 2" squares of tulip fabrics. I used 6 red tulips, 6 blue tulips, 4 white tulips, and 4 yellow tulips in the center of my quilt.

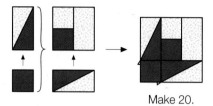

Make 20.

3. Sew a 2" x 2" square of background fabric to the tip of each green leaf half-rectangle unit. Press the seam toward the square.

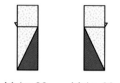

Make 20.   Make 20.

4. Draw a diagonal line across the back of each 6½" basket square. Place each basket square on one corner of the 11" background squares, right sides together; stitch along the pencil line. Trim ¼" from the seam line and press the seam toward the resulting triangle.

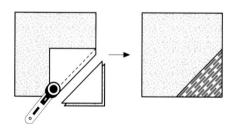

5. Sew a basket-weave triangle to one end of each 2" x 9½" background rectangle. Press the seams toward the triangle.

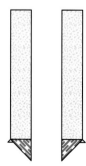

6. Arrange the tulips, leaves, basket, and background pieces for each of the 4 Basket blocks as shown below; sew them together.

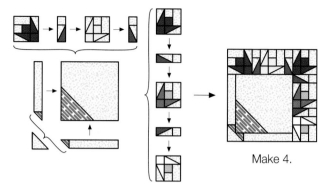

Make 4.

7. Cut the required number of leaves from dark green leaf fabrics using the patterns on page 125. From the green stem fabric, cut 20 bias strips, each ¾" wide. Fold each strip in half lengthwise, wrong sides together, and stitch ¼" *from the folded edge*. Insert a ¼" bias bar, roll the seam to the underside, and press. Remove the bias bar.

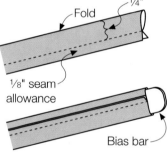

8. Referring to the quilt photo on page 31, arrange leaves and stems on the background block. Appliqué them in place. Undo a few stitches at the top of each basket and at the base of each tulip; tuck in the ends of the stems and leaves. Resew the seams.

9. Arrange the blocks as shown and sew them together in rows. Carefully pin the points that must match and stitch the 4 Basket blocks together.

Quilt Top Assembly and Finishing

1. Measure the quilt top for mitered borders. From the border fabric, cut 4 strips, each 2" x 38", for inner borders. Sew them to the quilt top, mitering the corners, and trim.

2. Sew each of 56 tulip 2" squares to a light green 2" square. Sew the pairs to-gether to make 28 four-patch units for the Tulip blocks.

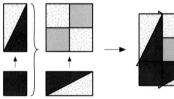

Make 28.

3. Arrange the four-patch units, tulip half-rectangle units, and 2" x 2" squares of tulip fabric as shown below to make 28 Tulip blocks. Sew the pieces together and press.

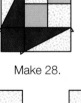

Make 28.

4. Sew each remaining leaf bias rectangle to a 2" square of background fabric as shown.

Make 12.   Make 12.

5. Arrange tulips and leaf rectangles as shown below and in the quilt photo on page 31 to make 4 borders.

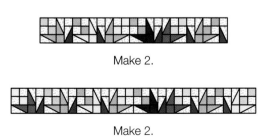

Make 2.

Make 2.

6. Sew the side borders to the side edges of the quilt top. Add the top and bottom borders to the top and bottom edges of the quilt top.

7. From the green border fabric, cut 6 strips, each 2" x 42", for the outer border. Cut 2 strips in half cross-wise and sew 1 piece to each of the remaining strips. Measure the quilt top for mitered borders. Sew them to the quilt top, mitering the corners, and trim.

8. Layer the quilt top with batting and backing; baste. Quilt as desired.

9. Add a hanging sleeve and a label to the back of the quilt. Bind the edges of the quilt.

I met Deirdre in
New Zealand in 1989
when we taught together.
Her Colourwash quilts
overwhelmed me, as did
the fact that she often
went for long five-mile
walks. Dan occasionally
accompanied her on the
walks, while I stitched
with her in the evenings.
Deirdre has a modest,
gracious personality and
is very easy to be with.
Her charming accent
puzzled me for several
days as I struggled to
figure out the name of
the second class she was
teaching, only to discover
that "appliqué" sounds
completely different
when another syllable
is accented.

—NJM

Colourwash Stripes and Rainbow Triangles

DEIRDRE AMSDEN

Deirdre is best known for her Colourwash quilts. She started making quilts in 1974 after attending an embroidery course at the Victoria and Albert Museum (London). Since 1987, she has concentrated on her Colourwash technique. In 1994 her book, *Colourwash Quilts: A Personal Approach to Design and Technique*, was published by That Patchwork Place.

Deirdre's work has been featured in many books and magazines and exhibited in Europe, America, New Zealand, and Japan. Teaching has also taken her to many countries, but home is a studio apartment in the east end of London.

Designer's Statement   This quilt was commissioned by Priscilla Miller and Asher Pavel of Chapel House/EZ Fabrics. They asked if I would like to make a quilt for them using their range of fabrics. The contrast between their ColorBars™ and print fabrics instantly appealed to me, so I agreed on the spot. Eagerly, I awaited the arrival of samples and fabric pieces from their designs both past and present. However, rinsing and pressing all this fabric during a London heat wave was not so pleasurable.

I visualized a design of bright colors, using the ColorBars fabrics, superimposed over a simple Colourwash design, using the prints. I settled on horizontal stripes for the Colourwash design and diagonal rows of brightly colored equilateral triangles, which would shade from purple to yellow to purple in a rainbow sequence and from light to dark to light within each color. I chose ten colors and eleven gradations, which created the right balance between the scale of the Colourwash stripes and the brightly colored rows of triangles. Directions are given for using ColorBars fabrics, but you may substitute other fabric if you wish.

Colourwash Stripes and Rainbow Triangles
by Deirdre Amsden, 1994
London, England
Finished Size: 62½" x 61"
Collection of Chapel House/EZ Fabrics

JUDY HOPKINS

Judy's sharp wit and low-key sense of humor have delighted Alaska quilters for years. She is a "Liberty Lady"—the Alaska winner in the Statue of Liberty contest. Those long Alaska nights (and a husband, Bill, who reads aloud to her as she quilts) are responsible for the many wonderful quilts she produces. Judy has developed a tradition of celebrating the shortest night of the year by staying up all night to quilt. Judy is always full of new ideas, like the Mystery! quilt pattern series she developed and markets.

—NJM

Judy is a prolific quiltmaker whose fondness for traditional design goes hand in hand with an unwavering commitment to fast, contemporary cutting and piecing techniques. Judy has been making quilts since 1980 and working full-time at the craft since 1985. Her work has appeared in numerous exhibits and publications.

Writing and teaching are by-products of Judy's intense involvement in the process of creating quilts. She is author of *One-of-a-Kind Quilts, Fit To Be Tied, Around the Block with Judy Hopkins,* and *Down the Rotary Road with Judy Hopkins,* and co-author with Nancy J. Martin of *Rotary Riot* and *Rotary Roundup.*

For the past several years, Judy has been working primarily from the scrap bag. Faced with a daunting accumulation of scraps and limited time with which to deal with them, she started looking for ways to apply quick-cutting methods to scrap fabrics. This led to the design of Judy's popular ScrapMaster ruler—a tool for quick-cutting half-square triangles from irregularly shaped scraps—and the accompanying blocks and quilts for the ScrapMaster book series.

Judy produces mystery-quilt classes for quilting groups, shops, and guilds, and mystery quilt patterns for individuals (through Feathered Star Productions). She also writes the regular Mystery! pattern series for *Lady's Circle Patchwork Quilts* magazine.

Judy lives in Anchorage, Alaska, with her husband, Bill, and their Labrador retriever. She has two grown daughters and two adorable and brilliant grandchildren who like to help her sew. Judy is active in her local guild, the Anchorage Log Cabin Quilters, and teaches regularly at Calicoes and Quilts Unlimited.

Designer's Statement   I have always had a special fondness for House blocks and quilts. The comfortable and familiar House pattern has been the jumping-off place for many of my experiments with color, value, and design.

Inspired by concepts taught by Michael James and Jan Myers-Newbury, this simple School House quilt combines traditional design with more contemporary value manipulation. The opposing light-to-dark gradations create a luminous glow.

School House Strip
by Judy Hopkins, 1995
Anchorage, Alaska
Finished Size: 23" x 53"

Materials: 44"-wide fabric

1 piece, 7" x 11", each of 10 yellow prints or solids of graduated values for blocks. Number these fabrics from #1–#10, with #1 being the lightest and #10 being the darkest.

1 piece, 7" x 11", each of 8 red-violet prints or solids of graduated values for blocks. Number these fabrics from #1–#8, with #1 being the lightest and #8 being the darkest.

⅛ yd. yellow print for middle border

1⅝ yds. red-violet print for inner and outer borders

27" x 57" piece of batting

1⅝ yds. for backing

⅜ yd. for binding

Cutting

All measurements include ¼"-wide seams.
From the yellow and red-violet color runs, cut:

Color	No. of Strips	Dimensions
Yellow		
1	4	1½" x 10½"
2	3	1½" x 7"
3	5	1½" x 7"
4	5	1½" x 7"
5	2	1½" x 7"
6	4	1½" x 7"
7	4	1½" x 7"
8	4	1½" x 7"
9	2	3" x 7"
	1	3½" x 7"
10	4	1½" x 10½"
Red-Violet		
1	2	1½" x 7"
2	4	1½" x 9½"
3	4	1½" x 9½"
4	4	1½" x 9½"
5	1	7" x 8½"
6	3	1½" x 7"
	1	2½" x 7"
7	3	1½" x 7"
	1	2½" x 7"
8	1	1½" x 7"
	1	6½" x 7"

From the yellow print, cut 3 strips, each 1¼" x 42", for the middle border.

From the *length* of the red-violet print, cut 3 strips, each 1¾" x 58", for the inner border, and 3 strips, each 5" x 58", for the outer border.

Block Construction

1. Make templates for the pattern pieces on page 127.

2. Join the yellow #9 and red-violet #1 strips to make 1 strip unit as shown. The strip unit should measure 10½" from raw edge to raw edge when sewn. From this strip unit, cut 4 segments, each 1½" wide, for the chimney section.

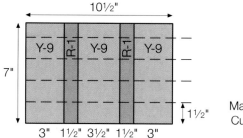

Make 1 strip unit.
Cut 4 segments.

3. Join the yellow #6, #7, and #8 strips to make 4 strip units as shown. The strip units should measure 3½" from raw edge to raw edge when sewn. Using Template A, mark and cut 1 piece with the template right side up and 1 piece reversed (template right side down) from each of these strip units for the sky section. The darkest of the yellow fabrics (#8) should be toward the top of the template.

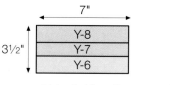

Make 4 strip units.

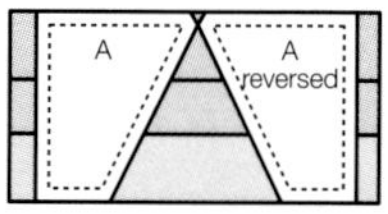

Cut 1 and 1 reversed from each strip unit.

4. Join the red-violet #2, #3, and #4 strips to make 4 strip units as shown. The strip units should measure 3½" from raw edge to raw edge when sewn. Using Template B, mark and cut 1 piece from each of these strip units for the roof section. Red-violet #2 should be toward the top of the template.

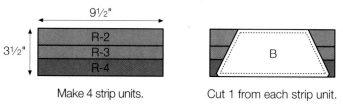

Make 4 strip units.

Cut 1 from each strip unit.

5. Join the pieces cut in steps 3 and 4 to make 4 sky/roof units as shown.

Make 4 sky/roof units.

6. Join the remaining strips to make the units shown below. Then cut into the required 1½"-wide segments as indicated.

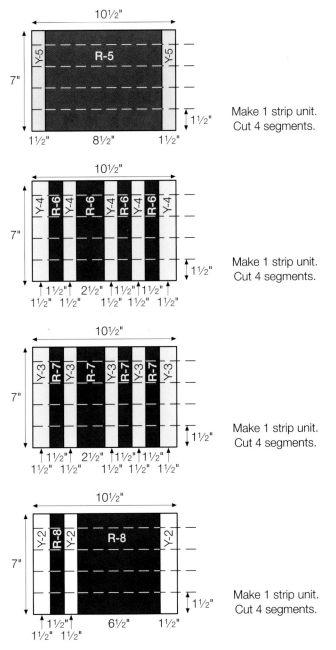

Make 1 strip unit.
Cut 4 segments.

Make 1 strip unit.
Cut 4 segments.

Make 1 strip unit.
Cut 4 segments.

Make 1 strip unit.
Cut 4 segments.

7. Arrange the units you have made with the remaining yellow #1 and yellow #10 strips and join them to make 4 House blocks.

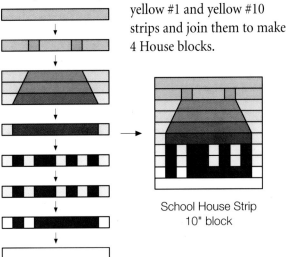

School House Strip
10" block

Quilt Top Assembly and Finishing

1. Arrange the blocks in a single vertical row as shown in the quilt photo on page 43. Join the blocks.
2. Measure the quilt top for straight-cut borders. Trim 2 of the 1¾"-wide red-violet print strips to fit the sides; sew to the side edges of the quilt top. Press the seams toward the border.
3. From the remaining strip, cut 2 pieces to fit the top and bottom; sew to the top and bottom edges of the quilt top. Press seams toward the border.
4. Repeat steps 2 and 3 to add the 1¼"-wide yellow print middle border (seaming strips as necessary) and the 5"-wide red-violet print outer border as shown in the photo on page 43.
5. Layer the quilt top with batting and backing; baste. Quilt or tie the quilt as desired or follow the quilting suggestion at right.

6. Add a hanging sleeve and a label to the back of the quilt. Bind the edges of the quilt with double-fold bias or straight-cut strips.

CAROL DOAK

What a bundle of energy and ideas! Carol's warm personality and great sense of humor delight quilters everywhere as she travels and teaches. This prolific quiltmaker is constantly submitting wonderful new manuscripts to That Patchwork Place. Carol uses a computer to draft and design her quilts, and she has even gone online with her own World Wide Web page (http://quilt.com/Artists/ Carol Doak/Carol Doak.html). I jokingly refer to her as the cyberquilter since she frequently communicates with other quilters by e-mail and quilt forums. She's usually available to answer questions and provide help.

—NJM

Carol is an award-winning quiltmaker, author, and teacher. She began teaching others how to make quilts in 1980 in Worthington, Ohio. Carol's teaching has taken her to many cities in the United States and recently to Australia to share her quiltmaking "Tricks of the Trade." She writes a column of the same title for *Quick and Easy Quilting* magazine. Her lighthearted approach and ability to teach have earned her high marks and positive comments from workshop participants.

Carol's quilts have been presented in several books, such as *Great American Quilts 1990* and *The Quilt Encyclopedia*. She has been featured in several national quilt magazines and her quilts have appeared on the covers of *Quilter's Newsletter Magazine, Quilt World, Quilting Today, Ladies Circle Patchwork Quilts* and *McCall's Quilting*.

Carol's first book, *Quiltmaker's Guide: Basics & Beyond* (AQS) was published in 1992. Her first book for That Patchwork Place, *Country Medallion Sampler*, was published in 1993. It combines a medallion-style quilt with a country theme. Carol's next book, *Easy Machine Paper Piecing*, set in motion a passion for designing foundation-pieced patchwork quilts. She used her paper-pieced block designs and quick foundation-pieced methods to create the garments featured in *Easy Reversible Vests*. Her next book, *Easy Paper-Pieced Keepsake Quilts*, features more paper-pieced quilts to treasure. Her latest book, *Easy Mix & Match Machine Paper Piecing*, offers innovative ways to combine paper-pieced patchwork and features fifteen exciting new quilts.

Carol lives with her family in Windham, New Hampshire, where the snow-filled winter months provide a pretty picture to contemplate as she keeps cozy under quilts in progress.

Designer's Statement   I designed this quilt to fulfill several goals. I wanted the quilt to be quick and easy to make and to symbolize the landmark anniversary That Patchwork Place celebrates in 1996. The twenty paper-pieced flower blocks were worked in shades of red and green against a beige background. The simple, three-piece geometric block was used to create a design that explodes in a star over a diamond on point. The flowers represent twenty years, the star represents the guiding impact of That Patchwork Place books, and the diamond represents the value of That Patchwork Place in the art of quiltmaking.

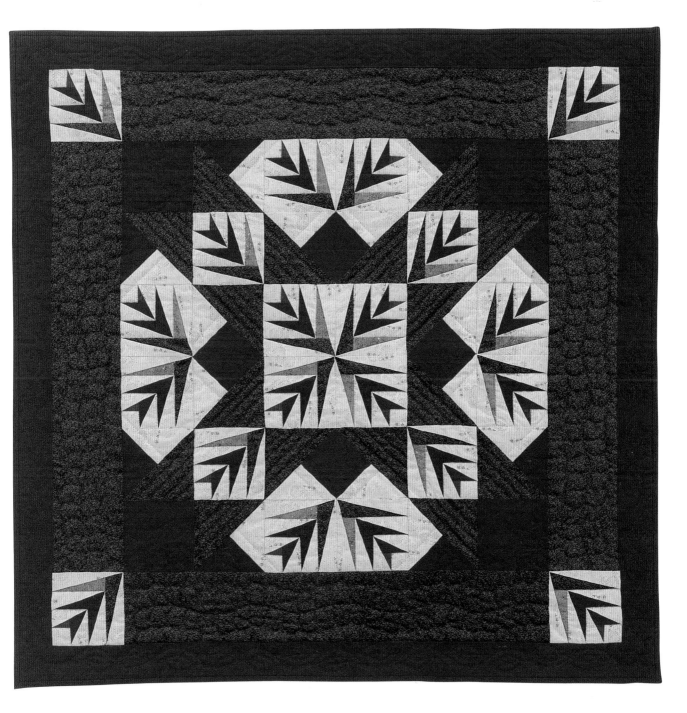

Floral Celebration
by Carol Doak, 1995
Windham, New Hampshire
Finished Size: 36½" x 36½"

Materials: 44"-wide fabric

- [ ] ⅞ yd. beige print for background
- [ ] ¾ yd. green #1 print for inner border and blocks
- [ ] ⅛ yd. green #2 print for blocks
- [ ] 1 yd. red #1 print for outer border, squares, blocks, and binding
- [ ] ⅛ yd. red #2 print for blocks
- [ ] ¼ yd. red #3 print for blocks
- [ ] ⅛ yd. red #4 print for blocks
- 40" x 40" piece of batting
- 1⅛ yds. for backing

Machine Paper Piecing

Machine paper piecing is a quick and easy method for creating precise patchwork. These hints will help you get started.

1. Make 20 copies of Block F41 and 16 copies of Block G3 on page 51, either by tracing the designs on transparent tracing paper and noting the numbers, or by photocopying them. If you choose to photocopy, be sure to use the same machine to make all photocopies for the quilt and use the original block designs in this book as your master. Trim the paper foundations ½" from the outside line.

2. Use a size 90/14 sewing-machine needle and set the stitch length at 18 to 20 stitches per inch. The larger needle and smaller stitch length will aid in the removal of the paper later.

3. Create a cutting and pressing area next to your sewing machine. Lower your ironing board and place a rotary-cutting mat on one end. Position a small lamp near the sewing machine to aid in fabric placement.

4. Make 1 block to confirm color choice and placement, then complete the remainder of the blocks in assembly-line fashion.

5. Once you complete the blocks and join them to other blocks and/or fabric, tug gently against the stitching to loosen, and remove the paper.

Cutting

Note: The cutting for Block A is under the Block A construction on page 49.

From the beige background print, cut:
4 squares, each 5½" x 5½". Cut each square twice diagonally for 16 quarter-square triangles; reserve for Blocks B, C, D, and E.

From the green #1 print, cut:
4 strips, each 4½" x 24½" for inner border
8 squares, each 5¼" x 5¼". Cut each square once diagonally for 16 half-square triangles; reserve for Blocks B, C, D, and E.

From the red #1 print, cut:
2 strips, each 2½" x 32½", for outer border
2 strips, each 2½" x 36½", for outer border
4 squares, each 4½" x 4½". Reserve for "Quilt Top Assembly and Finishing" on pages 50–51.
2 squares, each 5½" x 5½". Cut the squares twice diagonally for 8 triangles for Blocks D and E.

From the red #3 print, cut:
2 squares, each 5½" x 5½". Cut each square twice diagonally for 8 triangles for Blocks B and C.

Block Construction

Construct Blocks B, C, D, and E before you make Block A, since it is more complex.

Blocks B, C, D, and E

1. To construct Block B, select a G3 paper foundation. Place a beige quarter-square triangle, right side up, on the *blank* side of the paper over the piece #1 triangle space. Pin in place. Hold the foundation up to the light to make sure the fabric extends at least ¼" beyond the seam lines.

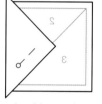

Looking at the blank side of the paper through to the lines on the other side

2. Place a red #3 quarter-square triangle, right side up, on the blank side of the paper over the piece #2 triangle space to confirm correct placement. Flip it, right sides together, with the piece #1 triangle along the adjoining seam. Again, be sure the fabric extends ¼" beyond the seam line.

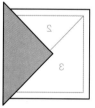

3. Holding the fabrics in place, lay the paper blocks, marked side up, under the presser foot and sew the first seam line between pieces #1 and #2. Extend the stitching for a few stitches beyond the beginning and ending of the line.

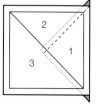

4. Trim the seam allowance to ¼". Open up piece #2 and press with a dry iron on a cotton setting.

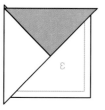

5. Add piece #3 (a green #1 half-square triangle), right sides together, across the first two. Again, be sure the fabric extends ¼" beyond the seam line. Sew the second seam line between pieces #1/#2 and piece #3. Open up piece #3 and press.

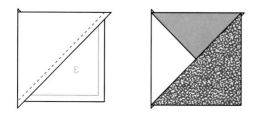

6. Use a rotary cutter and ruler to trim the edges of the block, leaving a ¼"-wide seam allowance beyond the outer lines of the marked design.

7. Make 3 more of Block B. Make 4 each of Blocks C, D, and E, placing the appropriate triangle pieces where indicated. Since the line drawing is actually the reverse of the block design, be sure to note the proper color placement on the *blank side of the paper*.

Block B
Make 4.

Block C
Make 4.

Block D
Make 4.

Block E
Make 4.

Block A

1. **From the beige background fabric, cut:**
   1 strip, 1½" x 32". Crosscut 20 squares, each 1½" x 1½" for piece #1.

Note: Follow the directions below to cut pieces #4, #5, #8, #9, #12, and #13 so they will open to the straight of grain:

For pieces #4 and #5, cut 2 strips, each 3" x 28", and place them right sides together. Place the F41 block design on the cutting mat and place a ruler along the seam line between pieces #3 and #4. Let the ruler extend onto the fabric as shown. Cut along the edge of the ruler to yield 1 piece each for pieces #4 and #5. Cut each piece so that the narrow end is ½" wide. Then cut a vertical line, allowing ½" at the bottom edge, to cut 2 more pieces. Continue to cut pieces across the layered strips, using the cut fabric piece as your pattern. Cut a total of 20 sets.

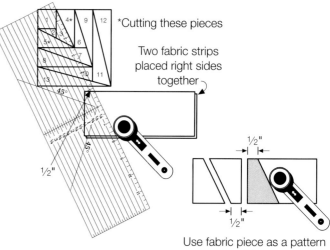

*Cutting these pieces

Two fabric strips placed right sides together

Use fabric piece as a pattern to cut additional pieces.

Cut 20 sets for pieces #8 and #9, using the same method. Cut 2 strips, each 4" x 28". Place the strips right sides together, and align the ruler on the line between pieces #6/#7 and #9.

For pieces #12 and #13, cut 2 strips, each 5" x 26". Place the strips right sides together, and align the ruler on the line between pieces #11 and #12. Cut 20 sets.

2. Cut the remaining pieces for Block A from strips:
   From the red #1, cut 20 pieces, each 4" x 1½".
   From the red #2, cut 20 pieces, each 3" x 1½".
   From the red #3, cut 20 pieces, each 3" x 1¾".
   From the red #4, cut 20 pieces, each 1½" x 1¼".
   From the green #1, cut 20 pieces, each 5" x 1¾".
   From the green #2, cut 20 pieces, each 4" x 1½".

Twenty Houses for Twenty Years

JOAN HANSON

JOAN HANSON

Joan began her love affair with fabric at an early age when her grandmother helped her make clothes for her dolls. She made her first quilt at the age of ten for her Barbie® doll. Her love affair with quiltmaking began in earnest in the early 1980s when she started making quilts using up-to-date techniques and equipment. One quilt led to another and one class led to another; before long, Joan was teaching classes on quilts she designed herself. Soon Nancy Martin asked Joan to write a book using her designs. Although she didn't own a computer and didn't type or spell very well, she responded that she would love to write a book. Thus, her first book, *Calendar Quilts*, came into being. (Then came the computer and a replacement for her twenty-five-year-old sewing machine.) One book led to others: *Sensational Settings—Over 80 Ways to Arrange Your Quilt Blocks* and, with co-author Mary Hickey, *The Joy of Quilting*.

For the past year, Joan, her husband, Jim, and their two sons, Derek and Mark, have lived through the extensive remodeling of their Seattle home. She is planning to start a Dust Support Group for other remodeling survivors. Joan can now be found in her newly expanded sewing studio, happily designing and stitching quilts that have lived, until recently, only in her imagination.

Designer's Statement House blocks have always been a favorite of mine, and it was the first idea that came to mind for a quilt to celebrate the twentieth anniversary of That Patchwork Place. Since its logo is a pieced House block, it seemed appropriate.

There are five different House blocks in this quilt. Several of the blocks contain two houses; that's how I managed to get twenty houses in sixteen blocks. These are very simple houses without chimneys or side roof pieces. There are even a few outhouses without windows! Each block has its own green base that forms horizontal sashing when the blocks are assembled.

It is appropriate that Joan chose a house theme for her quilt. Joan is my soul sister in remodeling and home-improvement projects. Her home economics background and strong color and design skills serve her well, but Joan doesn't stop at merely designing her home improvements; she gets involved in the hands-on work as well. I've seen her doing the woodwork for custom interior shutters, crafting a stone fireplace façade, laying a ceramic-tile floor, and stitching up loads of innovative window treatments. In addition, she makes tons of quilts, is a supermom to her two boys, and cooks and bakes in her gorgeous remodeled kitchen.

—NJM

Twenty Houses for Twenty Years
by Joan Hanson, 1995
Seattle, Washington
Finished Size: 42" x 42"

Note: I wanted this quilt to have a scrappy look. Sometimes it is harder to achieve this goal than it looks, but I found a method that worked. First I arranged the five different quilt blocks (on paper) into four rows of four blocks each to make a quilt plan. Then I cut all the pieces for the background and windows for each House block. Using the quilt plan as a guide and starting in the upper left corner, I chose fabrics for the first house and assembled it, then chose fabrics for the second house, so the colors and fabrics were evenly distributed throughout the quilt. As I completed each house, I added it to my design wall so I could stand back and check the colors. Occasionally, I flipped the placement of the door, window, and side pieces to vary the look of the block.

Materials: 44"-wide fabric

1 yd. tan print for background

¼ yd. each of assorted scraps of red, blue, green, gold, brown, and black prints (2 to 6 fabrics of each color) for houses

⅛ yd. print for windows

¼ yd. total assorted green prints for grass

46" x 46" piece of batting

2⅞ yds. for backing

½ yd. for binding

Cutting for Background

1. Make plastic templates using the triangle patterns on pages 129–30, or use the rotary-cutting dimensions given.

2. **From the tan background print, cut** 4 strips, each 2½" x 32½" along the lengthwise grain. Reserve them for the inner borders. You may choose to cut them longer and trim them to size.

Cutting for Houses

From the background, cut the following:

For House #1, cut:

4 squares, each 4⅞" x 4⅞". Cut the squares once diagonally for 8 triangles (Template #17).

8 rectangles, each 1½" x 3½" (#5)

For House #2, cut:

4 squares, each 3⅞" x 3⅞". Cut the squares once diagonally for 8 triangles (Template #19).

8 rectangles, each 1½" x 3½" (#5)

4 rectangles, each 1½" x 8½" (#9)

4 rectangles, each 2½" x 6½" (#11)

For House #3, cut:

4 squares, each 3⅞" x 3⅞". Cut the squares once diagonally for 8 triangles (Template #19).

8 rectangles, each 1½" x 4½" (#6)

4 rectangles, each 2½" x 7½" (#12)

For House #4, cut:

4 squares, each 2⅞" x 2⅞". Cut the squares once diagonally for 8 triangles (Template #21).

2 rectangles, each 2½" x 4½" (#10)

4 rectangles, each 1" x 3½" (#14)

4 rectangles, each 1" x 5½" (#16)

For House #5, cut:

4 squares, each 2⅞" x 2⅞". Cut the squares once diagonally for 8 triangles (Template #21).

2 rectangles, each 1½" x 4½" (#6)

2 rectangles, each 2½" x 4½" (#10)

4 rectangles, each 1" x 3½" (#14)

4 rectangles, each 1" x 4½" (#15)

From the print for windows, cut:

30 squares, each 1½" x 1½" (#2)

From the green prints, cut:

4 strips, each 1½" wide. From the strips, crosscut 16 rectangles, each 1½" x 8½", for grass (#9).

Cut several 1½"-wide strips from each of your fabrics for the houses and doors. From the strips, cut the pieces required in the following steps, using the dimensions given in the step-by-step directions. Reserve the leftover strips for the border. You will need some pieces wider than 1½"; reserve some fabric for these pieces.

Block Construction

Note: Because this project requires frequent pressing of short seams, set up an iron and ironing pad beside your sewing machine.

1. **To make the 4 House #1 blocks, cut** the following pieces from a variety of the fabrics for houses:

4 triangles for roofs (Template #18)

8 rectangles, each 1" x 1½" (#1), for houses

4 squares, each 1½" x 1½" (#2), for houses

4 rectangles, each 1½" x 2½" (#3), for houses

4 rectangles, each 1½" x 2½" (#3), for doors

4 rectangles, each 1½" x 4½" (#6), for houses

4 rectangles, each 1½" x 6½" (#8), for houses

2. Arrange the pieces with the required background and grass pieces; sew them together in the order shown.

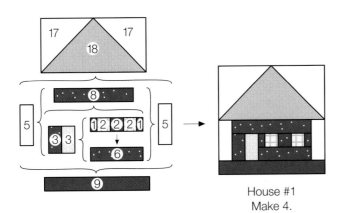

House #1
Make 4.

3. **To make the 4 House #2 blocks, cut** the following pieces from a variety of the fabrics for houses:

    4 triangles for roofs (Template #20)
    8 rectangles, each 1" x 1½" (#1), for houses
    8 rectangles, each 1½" x 2½" (#3), for houses
    4 rectangles, each 1½" x 2½" (#3), for doors
    4 rectangles, each 1½" x 4½" (#6), for houses

4. Arrange the pieces with the required background and grass pieces; sew them together in the order shown.

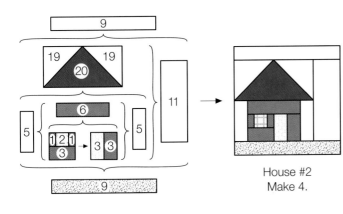

House #2
Make 4.

5. **To make the 4 House #3 blocks, cut** the following pieces from a variety of the fabrics for houses:

    4 triangles for roofs (Template #20)
    12 rectangles, each 1" x 1½" (#1), for houses
    8 squares, each 1½" x 1½" (#2), for houses
    4 rectangles, each 1½" x 2½" (#3), for doors
    4 rectangles, each 1½" x 3" (#4), for houses
    4 rectangles, each 1½" x 4½" (#6), for houses
    4 rectangles, each 1" x 2½" (#13), for houses

6. Arrange the pieces with the required background and grass pieces; sew them together in the order shown.

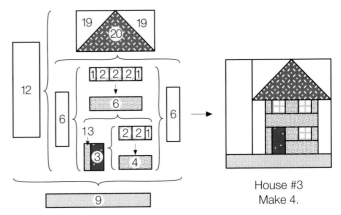

House #3
Make 4.

7. **To make the 2 House #4 blocks, cut** the following pieces from a variety of the fabrics for houses:

    4 triangles for roofs (Template #22)
    4 rectangles, each 1" x 1½" (#1), for houses
    4 rectangles, each 1½" x 2½" (#3), for houses
    4 rectangles, each 1½" x 2½" (#3), for doors
    2 rectangles, each 1½" x 3½" (#5), for houses
    4 rectangles, each 1½" x 5½" (#7), for houses

8. Arrange the pieces with the required background and grass pieces; sew them together in the order shown.

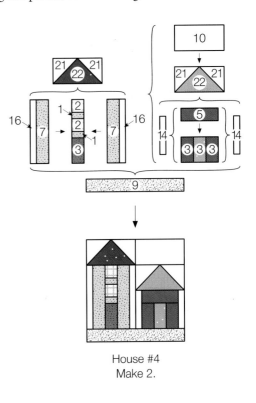

House #4
Make 2.

9. **To make the 2 House #5 blocks, cut** the following pieces from a variety of the fabrics for houses:

4 triangles for roofs (Template #22)
4 rectangles, each 1" x 1½" (#1), for houses
4 rectangles, each 1½" x 2½" (#3), for houses
4 rectangles, each 1½" x 2½" (#3), for doors
2 rectangles, each 1½" x 3½" (#5), for houses
4 rectangles, each 1½" x 4½" (#6), for houses

10. Arrange the pieces with the required background and grass pieces; sew them together in the order shown.

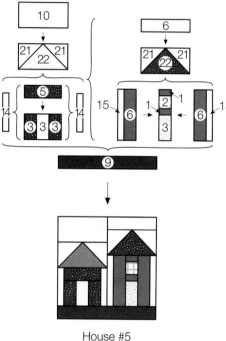

House #5
Make 2.

Quilt Top Assembly and Finishing

1. Arrange the blocks in rows as shown in the color photo on page 53. Sew the blocks together in rows. Press seams in opposite directions from row to row. Sew the rows together.

2. Measure the quilt top for straight-cut borders. Trim the reserved strips of background to fit the sides; sew to the side edges of the quilt top. Press the seams toward the borders.

3. From the leftover fabric for houses, roofs, and doors, cut 12 squares, each 1½" x 1½"; cut 4 squares from background fabric.

4. Arrange 1 background square and 3 assorted scrap squares as shown below and sew them together to make corner blocks.

Make 4.

5. Sew 1 block to each end of the remaining border strips. Check placement of the background square in each block. Press the seams toward the border strip.

6. Sew the borders to the top and bottom edges of the quilt top. Press the seams toward the borders.

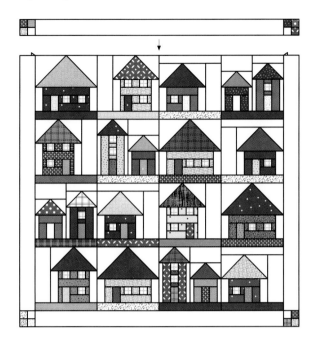

7. Cut the remaining 1½"-wide strips of scrappy fabrics, into 1½" x 12" strips. Sew the strips together in groups of 3. Press seams in one direction.

8. Cut the strips into 1½" segments. Cut 156 segments.

Cut 156 segments.

9. Sew the segments together in a random color arrangement to make 2 border strips with 36 segments and 2 border strips with 42 segments.

Make 2.

Make 2.

10. Sew the short border strips to the side edges of the quilt top. Press the seams toward the inner border. Sew the remaining border strips to the top and bottom edges of the quilt top. Press the seams toward the inner border.

11. Layer the quilt top with batting and backing; baste. Quilt as desired or see the quilting suggestion below.

12. Add a hanging sleeve and a label to the back of the quilt. Bind the edges of the quilt.

JUDY MURRAH

Judy learned to sew at an early age from her mother, and she's been exploring this creative medium ever since. With a degree in education and art from Southwest Texas State University, she taught her first quilt classes in Houston, Texas, in 1977. She now teaches classes on her original clothing and embellishment designs in South Texas fabric shops and at regional seminars and for quilt guilds throughout the country.

It's not surprising that Judy would soon find a way to meld her sewing background with her love for patchwork and write the award-winning book, *Jacket Jazz. Jacket Jazz Encore* followed quickly on its heels and is another best seller.

Judy continually experiments with patchwork and embellishment techniques to produce new and exciting designs that evolve into garments, quilts, and decorative items. She has just completed a third book, *More Jazz from Judy Murrah*.

Judy's growth as a professional instructor and author has paralleled her responsibilities as Director of Education with Quilts, Inc., in Houston, Texas. This organization produces six International Quilt Markets and Festivals each year, including the highly acclaimed International Quilt Festival in Houston each fall. Judy plans and coordinates jam-packed schedules of hands-on classes and lectures by guest instructors for all six affairs.

Although Judy's life sounds independent, it revolves around her family. She lives in Victoria, Texas, with her husband of twenty-nine years, Tom. They have three grown children: Todd, who is married to Julie; Holly; and Troy.

I've known Judy since I attended the first International Quilt Market in 1980. I always admired her quilter's wardrobe and the clever things she did with bits and pieces of lace, ribbon, and quilt blocks. Her garments were always fun to see, and in those days, we shared an affinity for the froufrou, ribbons-and-lace style.

In the early days of Quilt Market, activities were more informal, and some of the stunts we pulled resembled the antics you would see at Quilt Camp, rather than activities befitting a professional trade show. I have fond memories of Judy dancing to "Shimmy Like My Sister Kate." I also remember crazy Halloween pranks, including a ketchup-covered "dead body" in the hallway of the Shamrock Hilton Hotel.

—NJM

Designer's Statement   When That Patchwork Place asked me to be one of the contributors to this anniversary book, I was thrilled to have a reason to create a quilt in the Jacket Jazz style. Even though I had designed jackets, purses, Christmas stockings, and pillows in this way, I had not made a quilt. The process would be the same, but the end result would be flat, made to be placed on a wall rather than to conform to a curve or two.

As I pulled things from my stack and played with their arrangement, elements of the quilt took on a special meaning. The hearts are symbols for my three children, my husband, and myself. The Prairie Points include other members of my family. The clock and ribbon roses are a reminder to take time to smell the roses—part of living a long, healthy life. Even the touch of orange and yellow is part of the symbolism. The process became a personal journey of discovery.

From the Heart
by Judy Murrah, 1995
Victoria, Texas
Finished Size: 45" x 46"

Gathered Rosettes

1. Pin one end of ¼"-wide ribbon to the outside edge of the area you want to cover.
2. Thread a needle with a double strand of thread; knot. Anchor the ribbon to the fabric at the end with 2 backstitches. Anchor it again approximately 1" from the first anchor.

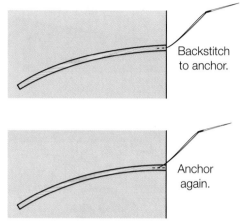

Backstitch to anchor.

Anchor again.

3. Lift ribbon away from fabric. Make a 1½"-long row of basting stitches through the center of the ribbon only.

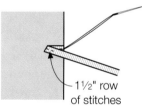

1½" row of stitches

4. Draw the thread up tightly to make a tiny gathered rosette. Anchor it through the fabric, close to the first anchor. Slide the thread under the fabric and anchor the ribbon at the next 1" interval.
5. Continue steps 3 and 4 until you come to the end of the area you want to embellish.

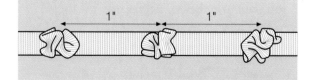

1"   1"

Draw up gathers to make roses, then tack to fabric strip.

Stitch and Slash

1. Cut identical pieces of 4 different fabrics and layer them one on top of the other. Pin the layers together. Draw a design of parallel diagonal lines on the top layer. The lines can be straight or curved. Stitch through all layers on each line.

2. Using a small, sharp pair of scissors and starting at a raw edge, cut through the top 3 layers of fabric between the lines of stitches. Do not cut through the bottom layer of fabric.

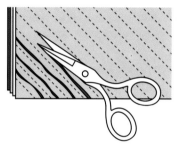

3. Wet the piece and dry it in the dryer. When it is dry, shake it to remove the loose threads.

Pleated Perfection

You will need the Perfect Pleater or EZE PLEATER designed to make ¼"-deep pleats. A pleater has stiff, permanent pleats (or tucks) into which you tuck your fabric. These pleats are called "louvers."

1. Cut a rectangle of fusible interfacing the desired size.
2. Select a piece of fabric and place it *right side down* on the pleater, with the bottom edge overlapping the pleater by 1".

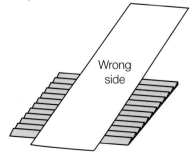

Wrong side

3. Firmly tuck the fabric into each louver, beginning with the one closest to you. Use a very thin metal or plastic ruler or a credit card to push the fabric completely into each louver before making the next pleat. Work from the center toward the outside edge of each row. Be sure the lower pleats do not become untucked as you make each subsequent pleat.

4. After you have made 6 to 8 pleats, steam-press them in place, pressing beyond the edges of the pleater, if necessary, to make a piece that is wide enough for the space you wish to cover on your quilt.

5. Hold these pleats in position by placing the lower portion of the fusible interfacing, fusible side down, on the pleats; fuse it in place.

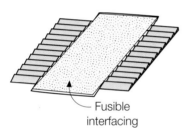

Fusible interfacing

6. Continue making pleats and fusing them to the interfacing after every 6 to 8 pleats until your pleated fabric is the desired size.

7. Cut your pleated piece to the desired size and shape, and add it to your quilt.

Magic Maze

1. Choose 7 high-contrast fabrics and cut a strip across the width of each one. The strips should vary in width but should total 11". When they are sewn together, they should be 8" wide.

2. Sew strips together using a ¼"-wide seam allowance.

3. Measure the width of the strip; use that measurement to cut squares from the strip.

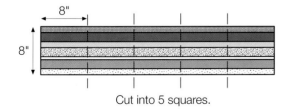

Cut into 5 squares.

4. Cut each square twice diagonally to yield 4 triangles. Label them A, B, C, and D.

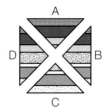

5. Arrange pairs of triangles as shown. Sew them together to make new pieced squares. Sew the squares together to make a strip and add it to your quilt top.

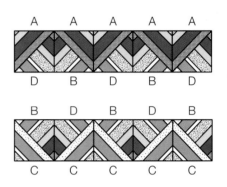

Zipper Piping

1. Choose a zipper from your collection and separate the two sides. Discard the pull, or save it to use as an embellishment if you desire.

2. Insert the fabric side of the zipper into one of the pleats of the pleated fabric so that only the teeth show. You may need to trim the fabric side of the zipper to fit.

3. Stitch the zipper into place, sewing on top of the pleat. See the illustration on page 61.

Prairie Points

1. Cut squares of assorted fabrics. You can use any size square; I used 2½" and 3½" squares.

2. For a Prairie Point with the fold on the edge of the triangle, fold the square in half diagonally, then fold the triangle in half again as shown.

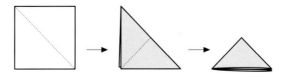

3. For a Prairie Point with folds in the center of the triangle, fold the square in half crosswise. Fold the top corners toward the center as shown below.

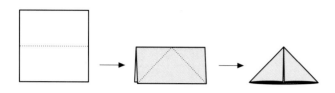

4. Insert the Prairie Point into a fold of fabric where desired and stitch it in place from the top of the fabric fold.

Seminole Patchwork

1. To make the Seminole design, cut 2 strips, 1½" x 42", 1 each from 2 coordinating fabrics. Cut 2 strips, each ¾" x 42", from a third fabric.

2. Sew 2 wide strips and 1 narrow strip together in the order shown below to make 1 strip set. Reserve the remaining narrow strip. Cut 1½"-wide segments from the strip set.

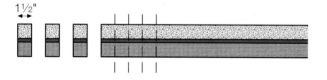

3. Sew half the segments to the remaining ¾"-wide strip. Cut them apart, keeping the edges parallel.

4. Sew the remaining segments to the other side of the narrow strip, keeping the colors in order.

5. From a background fabric, cut 2¾" x 42" strips as needed. Crosscut the strips at 2¾" intervals to yield 2¾" x 2¾" squares.

6. Sew a square to opposite sides of each Seminole square. Arrange the rows as shown below and sew them together.

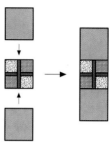

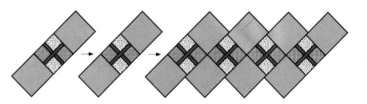

7. Trim the top and bottom edges ¼" away from the intersection of the background seams. Staystitch the long edges of the Seminole strip to prevent them from stretching.

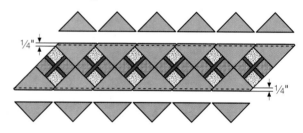

Edge Finishes

1. If you wish to add piping to the edges of a completed patchwork piece, allow ¼" extra at each edge when trimming excess. Stitch the piping to the right side of the piece. Use a zipper foot or cording foot so you can stitch close to the piped edge through the quilt top and fleece.

Stitch piping using zipper foot.

2. If you are using flat trim or gimp to cover the raw edges of the patchwork pieces, butt the edges of the adjoining patchwork pieces and zigzag over the raw

edges to hold them in place on the fleece. Center the flat trim or gimp over the raw edges. If you are using gimp, zigzag both edges in place. If you are covering raw edges with a flat braid or binding, straight stitch along both edges of the trim.

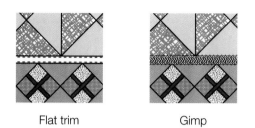

Flat trim　　　　　Gimp

Continuous Prairie Points

1. Cut strips of 4 different fabrics, each 4¼" x 42.
2. On the wrong side of 1 strip, mark a line ½" from the cut edge. This will become a band to hold the points together.
3. Stack 4 layers of fabric together with the marked strip on top, wrong side up. Using the rotary cutter, cut vertically every 4" through all layer, to the drawn line only. Separate the strips.

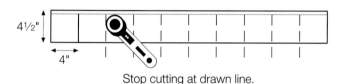

4½"
4"

Stop cutting at drawn line.

4. Fold and press each section of the strip diagonally, wrong sides together. The folding direction does not matter. Fold each section again diagonally.

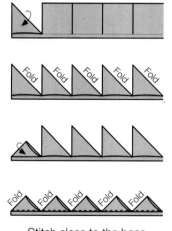

Stitch close to the base of the triangles.

5. Stitch close to the bottom edge of the triangles to catch the raw edges. Trim the edge ¼" from the stitching.

Quilt Top Assembly and Finishing

1. When you have completed the quilt top, trim the outer edges of the patchwork pieces even with the fleece and stitch ⅛" from the raw edges.
2. If you wish to add piping, stitch it to the quilt top before you add the Prairie Points. To add the Prairie Point border, place the raw edge of the border strip, right sides together, even with the raw edge of the quilt, and pin it in place. Trim away any unnecessary points. Stitch from the wrong side, following the stitching line of the piping.

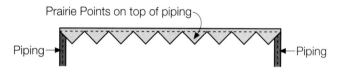

Prairie Points on top of piping
Piping　　　　　　　　　　Piping

3. Cut a piece of backing fabric the same size as the quilt top. Layer the quilt top, right sides together, with the backing; pin the edges securely. Stitch around the outside edge of the quilt, ¼" from the edge. Leave an 8"-long section open along 1 edge.
4. Trim the corners of the quilt top, then turn the quilt right side out through the opening. Smooth all the layers and carefully push out the corners. Slipstitch the opening closed.
5. Add beads, charms, buttons, fabric flowers, and other embellishments. Use the patterns on page 127 to appliqué hearts and teardrops if desired. Tack the quilt to the backing in several places to keep it from pulling away.
6. Add a hanging sleeve and a label to the back of the quilt.

Autumn Song

CAROLANN M. PALMER

Carolann, an enthusiastic quilt teacher and designer, is eager to share her unique patterns and ideas with others. She made her first quilt more than thirty-five years ago and has since made several hundred quilts for friends and family. She is the author of four books and a pattern packet for That Patchwork Place: *Branching Out—Tree Quilts, Baby Quilts from Grandma, Nifty Ninepatches, Quilts for Kids,* and *Garden Window.*

Carolann is also active in her quilting guild, Quilters Anonymous; the Seattle Quilt Troupe; and the Monday Night Bowling League (also a quilting group). She likes to cook and camp, but her favorite time is spent with her eight grandchildren.

Designer's Statement   Trees and quilts have always been a significant part of my life. I grew up in a small town in Oregon, and as a child, I regularly accompanied my mother as she went to help friends with their quilts. It was quite natural for me to love quilts and to make them.

Each summer, we took a two-week vacation, and we always spent it camping and hiking in one of our national parks. There were lots of tall trees, and I dearly loved to play in and around them.

I have always loved fall colors and this is reflected in many quilts I have made. "Autumn Song" is another in a series of tree quilts that bring together several favorite things in my life.

The trees sing out to me, and I can say with Isaiah of old, "Let all the trees of the wood shout for joy."

Carolann's lively sense of humor and fun personality delight all who come in contact with her. We first met in 1985 when Carolann served as president of our local guild, Quilters Anonymous, and I was vice-president. Carolann has been quilting for more than thirty-five years, and she loves making quilts for kids, including her eight grandchildren. She also makes a quilt to welcome every new baby into her church, more than two hundred quilts to date. As a member of the Monday Night Bowling League (a quilting group), Carolann regularly teased me about how much she hated to make bias squares, so I was shocked to see all those bias squares in her quilt!

—NJM

Autumn Song
by Carolann M. Palmer, 1995
Seattle, Washington
Finished Size: 48" x 48"

Materials: 44"-wide fabric

1¼ yds. off-white print for background
1 piece, 9" x 22", each of 5 rust prints for trees
⅛ yd. brown print for tree trunk
⅛ yd. dark tan print for ground
¼ yd. gold print for tree center and setting squares
⅓ yd. dark gold print for sashing
1⅓ yds. rust print for sashing, inner border, and binding
1¼ yds. large-scale print for setting triangles and corners
54" x 54" piece of batting
3 yds. for backing

Cutting

Cut all strips across the width of the fabric, on the crosswise grain.

From the off-white background fabric, cut:
   3 strips, each 9" x 42". Cut the strips in half crosswise to make 6 pieces, each 9" x 22". There will be 1 extra piece.
   1 strip, 6½"x 42". Crosscut 5 squares, each 6½" x 6½".
   2 strips, each 4½"x 42". Crosscut 10 squares, each 4½" x 4½".
   Trim the remainder of the 4½"-wide strip to 2½" wide and crosscut 5 squares, each 2½" x 2½".

From the gold print, cut:
   1 strip, 2½" x 42". Crosscut 10 squares, each 2½" x 2½", for tree centers.
   Cut 1 strip, 2½" x 42". Crosscut 12 squares, each 2½" x 2½", for setting squares.

From the brown print, cut:
   1 strip, 1" x 42", for tree trunks

From the dark tan print, cut:
   1 strip, 4½" x 42". Crosscut 5 squares, each 4½" x 4½", for ground.

From the dark gold print, cut:
   6 strips, each 1½" x 42", for sashing

From the rust print, cut:
   12 strips, each 1" x 42", for sashing strips
   5 strips, each 1" x 42", for inner border
   Cut the remaining fabric into 2½"-wide bias strips for binding.

From the large-scale print, cut:
   1 square, 22" x 22". Cut the square twice diagonally for 4 setting triangles.

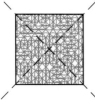

2 squares, each 14" x 14". Cut the squares once diagonally for 4 corner triangles.

Block Construction

1. Layer one 9" x 22" piece of background and 1 piece of tree fabric, *both right sides up.* Cut 2½"-wide bias strips. Alternating the fabrics, sew the strips into 2 larger units. Press the seams toward the tree fabric.

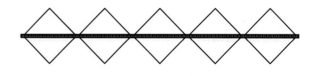

Make 2.

2. From these strips, cut 35 bias squares, each 2½" x 2½". See page 119.
3. Repeat steps 1 and 2 with the remaining 4 tree fabrics. Use 16 bias squares from each pair of fabrics to construct a Tree block. Reserve the remaining 19 bias squares for the pieced border.
4. To make the trunk unit, cut each of the 6½" x 6½" background squares once diagonally. Sew 1 triangle to each side of the 1" x 42" brown print strip. Be sure to align the triangles on opposite sides of the strip.

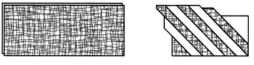

5. Press the seams toward the brown print strip. Cut the units apart and trim them to 6½" x 6½" squares.

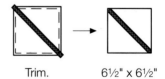

Trim. 6½" x 6½"

6. Draw a diagonal line on the wrong side of each 4½" dark tan square. Position a square over 1 corner of the tree trunk as shown; sew on the drawn line. Trim the square ¼" from the stitching; press the triangle toward the corner. Trim each square to 6½" x 6½".

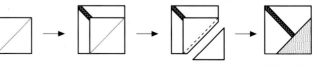

Make 5.

7. Following the block piecing guide below, arrange the pieces and sew them together in the order shown. Press seams as indicated below.

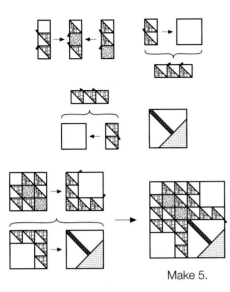

Make 5.

Quilt Top Assembly and Finishing

1. Sew the 1½" x 42" dark gold strips and the 1" x 42" rust strips together as shown below. Press the seams toward the rust strips. Crosscut the pieced strips at 12½" intervals to make sashing strips.

12½"

Cut 16.

2. Arrange the blocks, sashing strips, corner squares, and setting triangles as shown below. Sew them together in diagonal rows. Sew the rows together and add the corner triangles last.

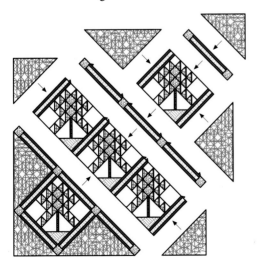

3. Sew the 5 remaining rust strips together, end to end, to make 1 long strip; crosscut into 2 pieces, each 1" x 42½", and 2 pieces, each 1" x 44½". Sew the shorter border strips to the side edges of the quilt top. Add the longer strips to the top and bottom edges of the quilt top. Press the seams toward the border.

4. Arrange 22 bias squares as shown below and sew them together to make 2 side borders. Make 1 top and 1 bottom border with 24 bias squares in each.

Make 2.

Make 2.

5. Add the shorter borders to the side edges of the quilt top; sew the longer ones to the top and bottom edges of the quilt top. Press the seams toward the narrow inner border.

6. Layer the quilt top with batting and backing; baste. Quilt as desired or see the quilting suggestion below.

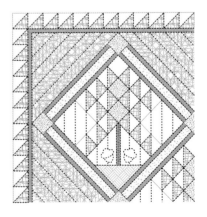

7. Add a hanging sleeve and a label to the back of the quilt. Bind the edges with double-fold, bias-cut strips of rust fabric.

69

Strawberry Patch

MIMI DIETRICH

Mimi lives in Baltimore, Maryland, with her husband and two sons. She has a degree in American Studies from the University of Maryland, Baltimore County. She is also one of the "founding mothers" of the Village Quilters and the Baltimore Appliqué Society.

Mimi specializes in teaching dimensional appliqué techniques in her Baltimore Album quilt classes. She has designed a "Home Town" tour of Baltimore, visiting monuments and other landmark places that are stitched into Album quilts. Her latest project involves quilt research at the Smithsonian Institution's National Museum of American History.

She is the author of *Happy Endings—Finishing the Edges of Your Quilt*, *Handmade Quilts*, *Baltimore Bouquets*, *Quilts from the Smithsonian*, and she is the co-author of *The Easy Art of Appliqué*.

Designer's Statement   To design "Strawberry Patch," I combined elements from some of my favorite quilt designs in my books published by That Patchwork Place. Because I live and teach in Baltimore, one of my favorite books is *Baltimore Bouquets*, and my favorite block pattern is the Strawberry Wreath. For this quilt, I thought it would be fun to stitch jumbo strawberries and make the blossoms a bit bigger. I also included dimensional, lined leaves that lift up to reveal a few friendly ants! Ladybugs and bumblebees also arrived to add to the fun.

The Strawberry Patch borders were inspired by two of my favorite border designs. I used the Garden Path border from the "Miniature Violets" quilt in *The Easy Art of Appliqué* and the Picket Fence border from *Handmade Quilts*. It also includes Prairie Points from *Happy Endings—Finishing the Edges of Your Quilt*.

Strawberries always remind me of parties at the beginning of summer, with wonderful fresh fruit salads and even better desserts! I hope you sense my feelings of fun and celebration as you create your own "Strawberry Patch" quilt.

Publishing Mimi's first book, Happy Endings, *certainly brought many "happy endings" to That Patchwork Place. We have yet to give Mimi her platinum book (like the platinum records that recording artists receive).*

She and her friend, Norma Campbell, have a delightful sense of humor and enjoy practical jokes. Their best prank happened when they led a Baltimore Album study group on a tour of that town's famous sights, including the baseball stadium, Camden Yard. They somehow managed to come away with a pair of autographed Jockey™ shorts from baseball player Jim Palmer, like those he models for the ads.

—NJM

Strawberry Patch
by Mimi Dietrich, 1995
Baltimore, Maryland
Finished Size: 43" x 43"

Sashing Strips and Borders

1. Sew a medium green piece B to each side of a light green piece A. Stitch a light green piece C to each side of a medium green piece D. Sew the resulting triangles to each side of a medium green piece E to make a setting square. Make 16 squares.

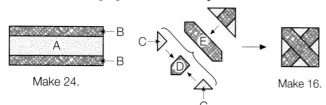

Make 24.   Make 16.

2. Sew sashing strips and appliqué blocks together as shown below to make 3 rows. Press the seams toward the sashing strips.

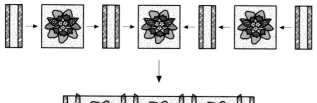

Make 3.

3. Sew sashing strips and setting squares together as shown to make 4 rows. Press seams toward the sashing strips.

Make 4.

4. Arrange the rows as shown below and sew them together to complete the quilt top.

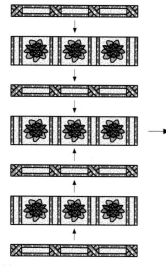

5. Sew the 1½" x 32½" dark green borders to opposite sides of the quilt top. Press these seams and all remaining seams toward the dark green border. Add the 1½" x 34½" dark green borders to the top and bottom edges of the quilt top.

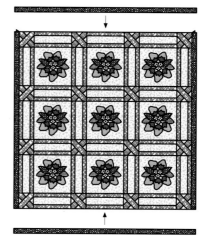

6. Sew a 2¼" x 42" medium green strip to each side of a 1½" x 42" white strip. Make 2 units. Crosscut each unit into 1½"-wide segments to make 52 "spaces" for the picket fence border.

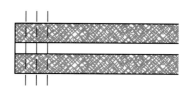

7. Alternate 14 white pickets (reserved from "Cutting," page 72) with 13 green-white-green spaces to make the borders. Repeat to make a total of 4 borders.

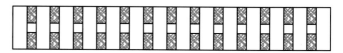

Make 4.

8. Sew a fence border to opposite side edges of the quilt top. Press the seams toward the dark green borders. Sew the 5" medium green squares to the ends of the 2 remaining fence borders. Sew these borders to the top and bottom edges of the quilt top.

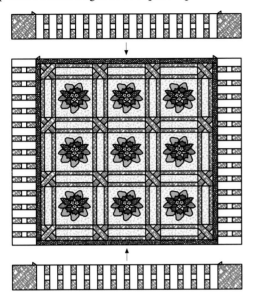

9. For the Prairie Points border, fold the reserved green and white 2" squares in half and press. Fold each side down toward the middle and press to make the Prairie Point.

10. Position the raw edges of the white points at the edge of each white picket strip, with the flat edge next to the front. The folds will be toward the back of the quilt when finished. Baste around the edges of the quilt to attach the white points.

11. Place the green points between the white points. Arrange 3 green points at the end of each row as shown, slightly overlapping them.

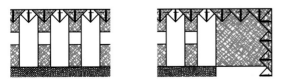

12. Sew the green points to the edges of the quilt. Insert the needle directly between the Prairie Points in the corner and pivot the quilt to stitch the next seam.

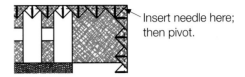

Insert needle here; then pivot.

Quilt Top Assembly and Finishing

1. Pin the quilt top and backing right sides together, sandwiching the Prairie Points between the top and back. Stitch around the outside edge, leaving an 8" opening on one side for turning. Trim the back of the quilt to match the front.

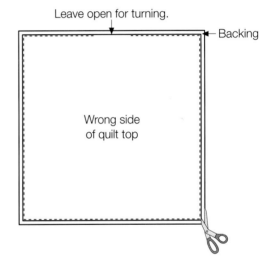

Leave open for turning.

Backing

Wrong side of quilt top

2. Place the quilt sandwich on the batting, with the quilt top next to the batting. Sew around the edges of the quilt to attach the batting, then trim it close to the stitching.

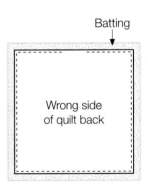

Batting

Wrong side of quilt back

3. Turn the quilt right side out and smooth it. Hand stitch the opening closed with small stitches. Baste the quilt top, batting, and backing together.

4. Outline-quilt around the appliqué and Garden Path sashing. Quilt on both sides of the narrow border and along the edges of the picket fence border.

5. Add a hanging sleeve and a label to the quilt back.

Connie and Mary are among my many long-distance good friends. I first met them in a scrap-quilt class I was teaching. After looking at their work, I wondered what they could learn from me. I encouraged them to write a book, and On Behalf of Chickens *was hatched. Several years later, we published a book about their successful quilt shop, Country Threads. Their books, patterns, newsletter, and shop are just as much fun as these two personable designers. When we renew friendships at the twice-yearly Quilt Markets, I can't wait to hear how Connie's cabin at the lake is progressing or the latest tale about Mary's animals.*

—NJM

Swing Your Partner

MARY TENDALL AND CONNIE TESENE— COUNTRY THREADS

Country Threads is located in a renovated chicken coop on a small farm in north central Iowa, surrounded by trees, shrubs and flowers as well as goats, chickens, ducks, geese, cats, and Mary's dog, Red. This peaceful setting is the inspiration and focus of the Country Threads look created by Connie and Mary.

Located just three miles west of Garner on U.S. Highway 18, the quilt shop provides shoppers with the latest in patterns, books, and notions, plus 3,000 bolts of fabric. There is a heavy emphasis on plaids, stripes, and checks in the collection. Country Threads also offers many services, including machine quilting, a fabric club, a newsletter, classes, quilt retreats, and an ever-expanding mail-order business that helps friends across the country get the latest patterns, fabrics, and kits from Country Threads.

Mary lives on the farm where Country Threads is located and enjoys collecting antiques and folk art; reading; caring for her lawn, garden, and the animals; and eating chocolate.

Connie lives in Garner with her husband, Roy, and their three boys. Gardening, reading, collecting primitive folk art, rug hooking, family pets, and pie are some of Connie's favorite things.

Designers' Statement   A repainted, remodeled, rejuvenated barn at Country Threads was the inspiration for the quilt we designed in honor of That Patchwork Place's twentieth anniversary. "Swing Your Partner" features pieced squares, a flag, a goat, a goose, trees, and a horseshoe for good luck, all pieced and appliquéd in the true Country Threads scrap tradition. Swing your partner, do-si-do, allemande left, and away we sew!

Swing Your Partner
by Country Threads, 1995
Garner, Iowa
Finished Size: 40" x 50"

Materials: 44"-wide fabric

1½ yds. assorted light background fabrics
1½ yds. assorted light prints for blocks
1 yd. assorted dark prints for blocks
⅓ yd. each of assorted red, black, brown, green, and blue
    prints for blocks
¼ yd. each of 2 different red prints for barn
⅛ yd. each of assorted orange, gold, and yellow prints
44" x 54" piece of batting
1½ yds. for backing
¼ yd. for binding
Black embroidery floss

Cutting and Block Construction

Scrappy Square Blocks

1. **From assorted colored fabrics, cut** 392 squares, each
   1½" x 1½".
2. Arrange 49 squares in 7 rows of 7 squares each.
   Repeat with the remaining squares to make 8 blocks.
3. Sew the squares together into rows, pressing seams in
   opposite directions from row to row. Sew the rows
   together.

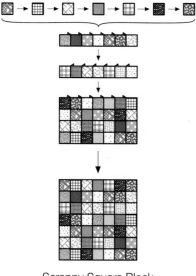

Scrappy Square Block
Finished size: 7" x 7"
Make 8.

Flag Block

1. Rotary cut the following pieces and arrange them as
   shown to make 1 flag block.

Piece No.	Color	Cut
1	Red	3 rectangles, each 1" x 8½"
2	Background	3 rectangles, each 1" x 8½"
3	Red	2 rectangles, each 1" x 12½"
4	Background	2 rectangles, each 1" x 12½"
5	Navy blue	1 rectangle, 3½" x 4½"

2. Sew the pieces together in the order shown.

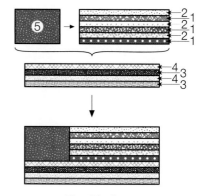

Flag Block
Finished size: 5" x 12"
Make 1.

Chicken Block

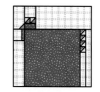

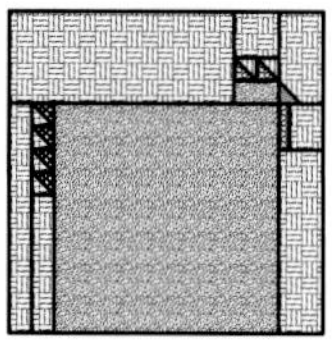

Chicken Block
Finished size: 7" x 7"
Make 1.

Chicken Block Reversed
Finished size: 7" x 7"
Make 1.

1. Rotary cut the following pieces. Use the same
   background fabric for pieces #1–#9.

Piece No.	Color	Cut
1	Background	2 rectangles, each 2½" x 5½"
2	Background	2 squares, each 1½" x 1½"
3	Background	2 rectangles, each 1½" x 2½"
4	Background	2 squares, each 1⅜" x 1⅜"; cut once diagonally for 4 half-square triangles
5	Background	2 rectangles, each 1¼" x 1½"
6	Background	2 rectangles, each 1½" x 4½"
7	Background	2 rectangles, each 1" x 3½"
8	Background	2 rectangles, each 1" x 5½"
9	Background	4 squares, each 1⅜" x 1⅜"; cut once diagonally for 8 half-square triangles
10	Beak	2 squares, each 1" x 1"
11	Comb	2 squares, each 1⅜" x 1⅜"; cut once diagonally for 4 half-square triangles
12	Wattle	2 rectangles, each ¾" x 1½"
13	Tail feathers	4 squares, each 1⅜" x 1⅜"; cut once diagonally for 8 half-square triangles
14	Body	2 squares, each 5½" x 5½"
15	Head	2 rectangles, each 1" x 1½"

2. Sew 4 background triangles (piece #4) to 4 comb triangles (piece #11). Sew 8 background triangles (piece #9) to 8 tail feather triangles (piece #13).

Make 4.　　　　　　Make 8.

3. Draw a diagonal line from corner to corner across each piece #10. Place a piece #10 on a piece #3 as shown and sew on the diagonal line. Trim ¼" away from the seam of piece #10 (do not trim piece #3) and press the triangle into position.

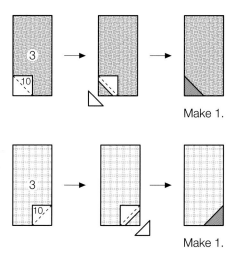

Make 1.

Make 1.

4. Referring to the illustration below, arrange all units as shown and sew them together to make 1 Chicken block. Reverse the arrangement to make 1 reversed Chicken block.

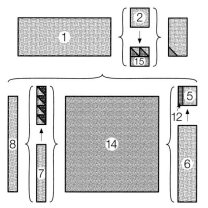

Star Block

1. Make templates for star pieces #1–#7 on page 134. Trace Templates #1–#3, #2 reversed, and #3 reversed on the wrong side of the background fabric; trace Templates #4–#7, #5 reversed, and #7 reversed on the red. Cut out all pieces.

2. Arrange pieces and sew them together in the order shown to complete 1 star block.

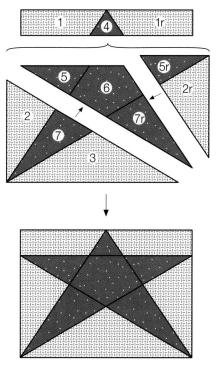

Star Block
Finished size: 5" x 7"
Make 1.

Barn Block

1. Rotary cut the following pieces:

Piece No.	Color	Cut
1	Red	2 rectangles, each 2" x 6½"
2	Red	4 rectangles, each 2" x 2½"
3	Red	4 rectangles, each 2" x 3"
4	Red	2 rectangles, each 1" x 6½"
5	Red	2 rectangles, each 1½" x 6½"
6	Red	1 rectangle, 2½" x 4½"
7	Red	2 rectangles, each 2½" x 4½"
8	White	4 squares, each 2" x 2"
9	Blue	1 rectangle, 1½" x 6½" (silo)
10	Blue	1 rectangle, 4½" x 5½" (silo)
11	Background	1 rectangle, 3½" x 16½"
12	Background	1 rectangle, 10½" x 13½"
13	Background	1 rectangle, 4½" x 5½"
14	Background	1 rectangle, 2½" x 16½"
15	Blue	1 rectangle, 2½" x 5½"
16	White	2 rectangles, each 1" x 3½"
17	White	2 rectangles, each 1" x 8½"
18	Red	2 rectangles, each 1" x 3½" (flag)
19	Red	2 rectangles, each 1" x 8½" (flag)
21	White	2 rectangles, each 1½" x 2½"

2. Make a template for piece #20 (page 136) and cut 1 and 1 reversed from red barn fabric.

3. Arrange pieces #1–#9 for the lower section of the barn and silo; sew them together as shown.

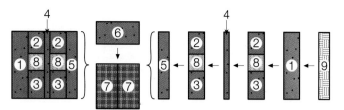

Lower Section of Barn and Silo

4. Arrange pieces #10, #12, and #13 as shown and sew them together to make the silo unit.

Make 1.

5. Arrange pieces #15–#19 for the flag and sew them together as shown.

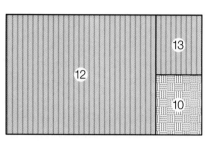

Make 1.

6. Add piece #20 and #20R to the sides of the flag. Align the bottom edges and trim the top edge of the flag as shown. Align the left edge of the barn roof with the left edge of the silo unit completed in step 4 above. Pin in place and appliqué. Appliqué the windows, using piece #21.

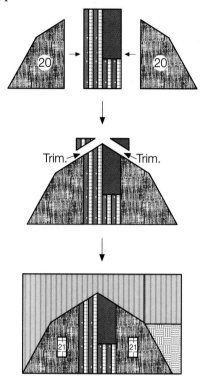

Appliqué to background.

7. Sew the upper and lower sections of the barn together and add side pieces #11 and #14.

8. With black floss, stitch "Iowa" on the silo.

9. Using Templates #22 and #23 on page 136, cut and appliqué the star and silo top.

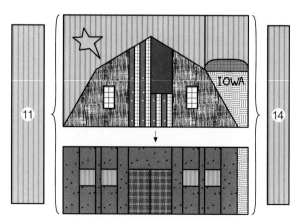

Appliqué Blocks

Make 1.

Tree #1
Make 1.

Tree #2
Make 1.

Tree #3
Make 1.

Rooster
Make 1 and
1 reversed.

Horseshoe
Make 1.

Heart
Make 1.

Goat
Make 1.

Goose
Make 1.

1. From assorted background fabrics, cut the following appliqué foundation blocks:

Rooster	2 squares, each 7½" x7½"
Heart	1 rectangle, 7½" x 8½"
Goat	1 square, 7½" x 7½"
Goose	1 square, 7½" x 7 ½"
Horseshoe	1 rectangle, 7½" x 9½
Tree 1 and 2	2 rectangles, each 7½" x 11½"
Tree 3	1 rectangle, 8½" x 14½"
Swing Your Partner	1 rectangle, 4½" x 22½"

2. Make templates for the patterns on pages 135–41. Cut the pieces from the desired fabric and appliqué them to the backgrounds as shown above.

3. Apply fusible web to the wrong side of the "Swing Your Partner" fabric. Place the letter templates right side down on the paper backing, trace them, and cut them out. Fuse them to the background rectangle.

4. Appliqué around each letter with the buttonhole stitch, either by hand or by machine.

Quilt Top Assembly and Finishing

1. From the assorted background fabrics, cut 1 each of the following spacer pieces:
   3½" x 5½"
   3½" x 7½"
   2½" x 7½"

2. Arrange all blocks and spacers as shown in the quilt photo on page 77 and sew them together.

3. From the assorted red fabrics, rotary cut 164 squares, each 1½" x 1½". From the assorted light prints, cut 164 squares, each 1½" x 1½". From the assorted green fabrics, cut 4 squares, each 2½" x 2½".

4. Sew red and light squares into pairs. Join pairs to make 2 rows with 36 pairs and 2 rows with 46 pairs. Sew a cornerstone to each end of the longer borders.

Make 2.

Make 2.

5. Sew the short borders to the top and bottom edges of the quilt top, then sew the longer ones to opposite side edges of the quilt top.

6. Layer the quilt top with batting and backing; baste. Quilt as desired.

7. Add a hanging sleeve and a label to the back of the quilt. Bind the edges of the quilt with straight-grain strips of fabric.

Confluence

MARGARET J. MILLER

Margaret is a studio quiltmaker who travels widely, giving lectures and workshops on color and design. Her full teaching schedule has taken her throughout the United States, as well as to Australia, New Zealand, South Africa, and Denmark. She is known for her enthusiasm, humor, and sincere encouragement of quiltmakers of all levels of skill and experience.

Having done various forms of needlework throughout her life, Margaret learned to quilt and appliqué in 1978. At that time, she was on the faculty of the home economics department at California Polytechnic State University, San Luis Obispo, teaching a creative textiles class. She later moved to San Diego, where she started Tanglethread Junction, a pattern business featuring appliqué and stained-glass appliqué designs. In 1982 she sold her business as part of her commitment to becoming a full-time quiltmaker.

In addition to *Blockbender Quilts*, on which her quilt "Confluence" is based, she is the author of *Blockbuster Quilts* and *Strips That Sizzle*. She also wrote the chapter on the Bloomin' Quilt Grids design technique in *Quilt with the Best* (Oxmoor House).

Margaret lives near Seattle, Washington, with her husband in a newly emptied nest. Her two sons, one a theater arts graduate and the other a sailor in the U.S. Navy, keep the nest from being empty for too many weeks at a time.

She is frequently accompanied in her studio (which, for the previous occupants of the house, was the formal living and dining rooms) by two cats and a boxer named Cal, who keeps the whole household laughing.

What a dynamo! Margaret is a high-energy, on-the-go quilter, whose positive attitude empowers the students she teaches. She encourages her students to "reach for the unexpected." I appreciated this attitude when I scheduled Margaret as the evening speaker at the first That Patchwork Place University. The theme for Margaret's speech and the show-and-tell that followed was "Pajama Party," so Margaret and I cast professional dignity and quilters' wardrobes aside and showed up for her presentation in robes, slippers, and hair curlers. Margaret refuses to relinquish the negatives for the photos taken.

—NJM

Designer's Statement   This quilt is the direct result of making sixty fabric mock-ups for my most recent book, *Blockbender Quilts*. Mock-ups enable me to experiment with color and value and create numerous quilts in a short period of time (especially when the deadline looms near). While experimenting with the design element of "borders within borders," I stumbled onto the plan for this quilt. I could hardly wait for the *Blockbender* manuscript and all of its attendant details to be finished so I could make this quilt for real. My current quilts are part of a continuing study in using a complete range of values, as well as including areas of both high and low contrast in any given quilt.

The process of writing the book showed me that the *Blockbender Quilts* idea is even more versatile than I dreamed. This is the first of quite a long series of Blockbender quilts that I look forward to creating.

Confluence
by Margaret J. Miller, 1995
Woodinville, Washington
Finished Size: 48½" x 50½"

5. Press the seam allowances in one direction in all the even-numbered rows; press the seam allowances in the opposite direction in all odd-numbered rows.

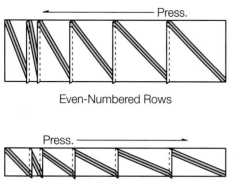

Even-Numbered Rows

Odd-Numbered Rows

Note: You may press seam allowances open as you did for the diagonal seams if you prefer.

6. To make a pieced quilt backing, cut 1¾ yards of fabric in half lengthwise. Sew a piece to either side of another fabric (or combination of fabrics) that measures 12" x 63". This will yield a backing larger than the top to accommodate basting and quilting.

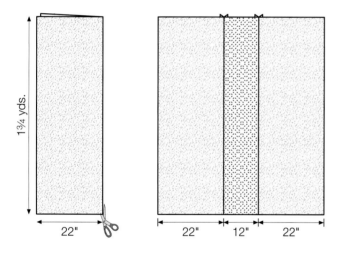

7. Layer the quilt top with batting and backing; baste. Quilt as desired or follow one of the quilting suggestions at right. Quilt designs are more effective for this quilt if they meander across triangles, following the pathways of light, rather than simply outlining the triangles.

8. Add a hanging sleeve and a label to the back of the quilt. Bind the edges of the quilt.

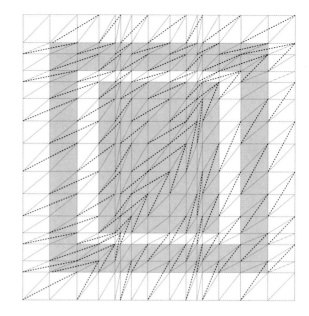

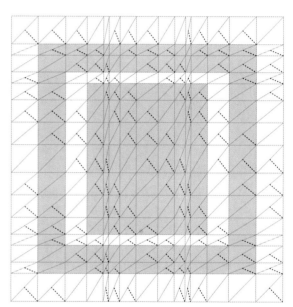

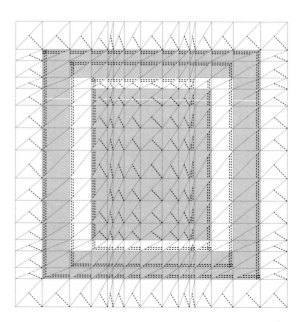

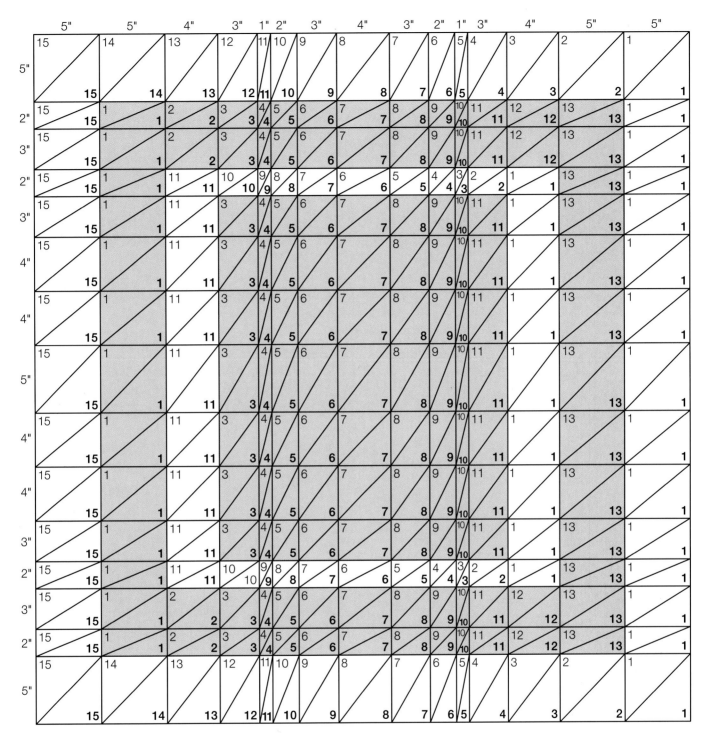

The dimensions around the outside of the quilt plan indicate the size of the row or column; the numbers on the inside indicate value. Refer to step 3 under "Cutting" on page 84.

Drink the Living Water

PAT MAIXNER MAGARET

I first became acquainted with Pat's work when her quilt, "The Third Day," was presented in Quilter's Newsletter Magazine. *Not long after, her quilt, "The Hills Are Alive," won the grand prize in the first That Patchwork Place Quilt Contest in 1991. Her artistic eye and excellent workmanship make all her quilts worthy of prizes, and her development of the watercolor technique with friend and co-author, Donna Slusser, has added a whole new dimension to quiltmaking.*

—NJM

Pat is a contemporary quiltmaker whose work is rooted in tradition. She particularly enjoys the design process and the use of unpredictable color combinations. She often combines appliqué with pieced work because she likes the way the straight and curved lines blend to enhance each other.

Pat's quilts have won awards at regional and national competitions, and her work has been published in numerous books and magazines. She has been teaching, lecturing, and serving as a quilt judge since the late 1980s. She team teaches with her friend, Donna Slusser. Together they have authored the books *Watercolor Quilts, Round Robin Quilts: Friendship Quilts of the '90s and Beyond,* and *Watercolor Impressions.* They have also designed a line of fabrics for South Sea Imports.

Pat graduated from the University of Nebraska with a degree in medical technology. She retired from that career when she started her family. Her other interests include gardening, music, and jogging daily with her dog. Pat lives in Pullman, Washington.

Designer's Statement   I have a special garden birdbath with little statuary birds that sit on it and sip even after real-life birds have migrated south. I especially enjoy watching it in midsummer, when the birds that visit are numerous and the flowers at its base are prolific. This watercolor quilt depicts that scene. It also speaks to my faith and is a reminder of our need to drink the Living Water that satisfies the thirst of our souls.

Drink the Living Water
by Pat Maixner Magaret, 1995
Pullman, Washington
Finished Size: 47" x 50"

Materials: 44"-wide fabric

Note: Read through the "Glossary of Watercolor Terms" on page 93 before you make this quilt, especially if you have never made a watercolor quilt before. In addition, you might also want to read *Watercolor Quilts* or *Watercolor Impressions*.

Assorted fabric scraps for appliquéd birds
1¼ yds. for inner border
1½ yds. for outer border
53" x 56" piece of batting
2⅞ yds. for backing
½ yd. for binding
Design wall
In addition, you will need a minimum of 675 assorted squares, each 2" x 2", cut from a wide variety of fabrics. Use various colors in a wide range of values. Within this assortment, include:

> Approximately 190 squares that contain parts of floral petals on a medium dark or dark background.

> Approximately 80 squares that contain "reachy" elements on a light background.

> Approximately 190 squares that have a smooth texture with impressions of pale color ("smoothy squares"). These need to be light in value. (The back side of many light floral squares can be used to create the smooth effect.)

You will need additional squares as your design develops.

Construction

Note: The fabrics shown in the photos on pages 90–91 may differ a little from the finished quilt on page 89.

1. On your design wall, build a watercolor birdbath using dark squares as shown. The birdbath is 19 squares wide by 15 squares long.

2. Fill in around the bowl of the birdbath with reachy squares to create a curve.

3. Near the bottom of the quilt, create flowers with squares that contain individual petals on dark backgrounds.

4. Complete the edges of the flower garden by adding reachy squares to create vines and tendrils for a soft and fernlike look.

5. Surround the open area around the birdbath with smoothy squares to create a glow.

6. Gradually add darker squares at the top to complete the design. Add reachy squares and build flowers; create the illusion of hanging vines if desired.

Quilt Top Assembly and Finishing

1. Carefully pick up the squares row by row (vertically) and sew them together. Take care that you do not mix them up or rotate them. Place a pin in the first square of each row as a marker to help you remember where a new row begins.

2. Press seams carefully with a dry iron. Press seams up in odd-numbered rows; press seams down in even-numbered rows.

3. Sew the rows together, matching the seams and carefully pinning them together before you sew.

4. Alternate the direction in which you sew seams from row to row to prevent the quilt top from appearing warped.

5. Make templates for the bird appliqués from the patterns on page 142. Cut each appliqué motif from the chosen fabric; appliqué the birds in place. The numbers on the appliqué pattern pieces refer to the order of appliqué. If desired, add details such as eyes, legs, shadows, and shading on the wings with a permanent marking pen. Always test the marker first on another scrap of the same fabric.

6. From the inner border fabric, cut 4 strips, each 1" x 42", cutting along the lengthwise grain.

7. From the outer border fabric, cut 4 strips, each 4½" x 54", cutting along the lengthwise grain.

8. Sew each inner border strip to an outer border strip, matching center points. These 2 strips will now be treated as 1 border.

9. Measure the quilt through the center for mitered borders. Sew the borders to the quilt top, mitering the corners.

10. Layer the quilt top with batting and backing; baste. Quilt as desired or stitch in-the-ditch around all the appliqué motifs and quilt random or free-flowing curved lines in the background. Outline-quilt around the created flowers and along the tendrils and vines to give dimension.

11. Add a hanging sleeve and a label to the back of the quilt. Bind the edges of the quilt.

GLOSSARY OF WATERCOLOR TERMS

Freckle Fabrics: These small- to medium-scale patterned fabrics contain both light and dark values as well as colors and lines that have a fair amount of contrast. Look for dark backgrounds with light patterns and light backgrounds with dark patterns. Use them to create a relatively smooth transition in a short amount of space.

Mooshing: A term for blending colors, values, and printed designs. When the design is viewed from a distance, the eye should flow along the piece without stopping on specific squares or edges. Achieve this effect by working with value and individual colors to carefully control the gradual blending.

Petal Squares and Creating Floral Blossoms: When you cut up large-scale prints, only parts of petals, leaves, and other fragmented images remain. Use the colors and lines in these squares as building blocks. Group several petals from similar-colored squares of different fabrics to create new blossoms. Make sure they all have a similar background value.

Reachy Fabrics: These have a plain or solid-looking background with lines and colors that resemble vines, branches, leaves, or flowers extending into space. Those printed on a lighter background are the most useful.

Smoothy Squares: These print fabrics have an absence of design lines, giving them a smooth appearance. They are the kinds of prints with no marks or strokes or other distracting patterns, just gentle, gradual shifts from one color to another.

Transition Fabrics: Reachy and freckle fabrics are used to form a bridge between areas of contrast. They help smooth out the stark lines between the birdbath and background in "Drink the Living Water" (page 89), and they help make the vase in "Summer's Song" (page 95) blend into the flower bouquet, as well as soften the area between the bouquet and the background.

93

Summer's Song

DONNA INGRAM SLUSSER

Donna grew up in the Portland, Oregon, area, where she learned to appreciate all the wonders of life: nature, art, books, music, and people. After graduating with a degree in education, she taught elementary school for several years.

She and co-author Pat Magaret have written three books for That Patchwork Place: *Watercolor Quilts, Round Robin Quilts: Friendship Quilts of the '90s and Beyond,* and *Watercolor Impressions.* Her expertise at designing and making wonderful quilts with 2" squares is legendary.

Donna lives high atop one of the hills of Palouse country in Eastern Washington State with her husband, Lloyd, and a menagerie of pets. She has three grown children and a new granddaughter. She enjoys music and gardening, both of which are frequent subjects of her quilts.

Designer's Statement   Watercolor quilts are created by using small squares of fabric to produce color effects, texture, and value shading in a quilt. It is similar to the technique used by the Impressionist painters in the latter part of the nine-teenth century. They placed dabs of paint side by side on their canvasses instead of mixing the paints on their palette. These dabs then blurred and blended in the eye of the beholder and became a beautiful painting. Watercolor quilts look like a hodgepodge of squares when viewed up close, but from a distance, the textile images mingle in the viewer's eye to become a lovely whole.

I love flowers—all sizes, colors, and varieties. What fun it is to play with 2" squares and make a summer arrangement of my favorite flowers to enjoy all year 'round. This bouquet is not too difficult for an experi-enced watercolor quilter or even a confident beginner.

If you want to stretch your creativity, change the size of the design, fashion a different vase, or change the blossoms to fit a different season. Consider creating "Spring Fling," "Autumn Splendor," or "Winter Wonder-land." Why not try a bouquet centered around a holiday theme, such as "Red, White, and Blue Splash," "Valentine's Day Wish," or "May Day Nosegay"? There are many flowers out there just waiting to be arranged in your favorite vase and stitched into a watercolor quilt!

Donna's artistic nature and gentle sense of humor are appreciated by her students. Ever compassionate, during a class at That Patchwork Place University, she and her friend and co-author, Pat Magaret, called the local pizza store to deliver two large pizzas and twenty empty boxes for the hard-working, hungry students. The empty boxes were for the students to store all of their 2" squares! I was sure Watercolor Quilts *would be a best seller when Kathy Poole, a member of the Monday Night Bowling League (a quilt group), shared her watercolor quilt with other members of the group. I knew anything that could produce open-mouthed dead silence for the Bowling League had to be a winner.*

—NJM

Summer's Song
by Donna Ingram Slusser, 1995
Pullman, Washington
Finished Size: 41" x 44"

Materials: 44"-wide fabric

Note: Read the "Glossary of Watercolor Terms" on page 93 before you make this quilt, especially if you have never made a watercolor quilt before. You may also want to refer to *Watercolor Quilts* or *Watercolor Impressions*.

1⅜ yds. for border
47" x 50" piece of batting
1½ yds. for backing
½ yd. for binding
Design wall

In addition, you will need a minimum of 624 assorted squares, each 2" x 2". Choose various colors in a wide range of values. Within this assortment, include:

Approximately 80 squares that contain "reachy" elements on a light background. These squares contain vining-type elements as well as some empty background space.

Approximately 150 squares that contain parts of floral petals on light, medium, or dark background (called "petal squares").

Approximately 375 squares of light value to be used as background. These squares have a smooth texture with impressions of pale color ("smoothy squares"). The back side of many light floral squares can also be used to create the smooth effect.

28 squares for the vase. Cut these from 1 fabric or a variety of fabrics.

Construction

1. Sort the squares by value. In addition to light, medium, and dark values, sort additional squares into the following 2 categories: reachy and petal.

2. On your design wall, create the largest blossoms in the center at the lowest part of the bouquet. Floral designers try to have an uneven number of blossoms in this part of the bouquet, but it is not necessary to adhere to this rule. Use squares that contain petal colors you want to have in your design. These "marker blossoms" form the base of your design, but remember that you may change their color, shape, or placement later. Blossoms in this part of the design should be darker, brighter, and more open than other flowers in the bouquet. Play with the blossoms until you find a pleasing arrangement.

Note: The fabrics shown in photos on pages 96–97 may differ a little from the finished quilt on page 95.

3. Fill in behind the marker blossoms with squares containing parts of floral motifs, leaves, and other flowers. Choose flower motifs that are lighter and smaller as you work your way into the upper parts of the design. When the arrangement is approximately 13 squares wide by 11 squares tall, add spike-type flowers. These resemble snapdragons, delphiniums, and other floral branches. Use reachy fabrics at the end of these spikes so they appear to trail off.

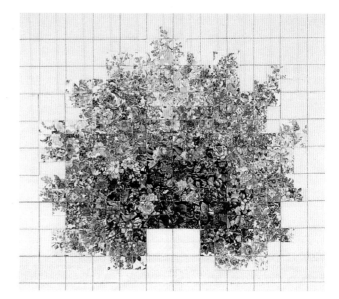

4. Fill in the blank spaces in the arrangement with additional small flowers. Add additional reachies around the outer edges to give the appearance of baby's breath or ferns and to add softness.

5. Arrange 28 squares to make a vase. To eliminate the straight line between the large blossoms of the bouquet and the vase, replace the 4 squares in the top row of the vase with squares that contain smaller flowers. Choose floral motifs that are on backgrounds which blend values and colors between the bouquet and the vase. I also replaced 2 additional squares on the left side of the vase with squares that have small flowers to give an asymmetrical appearance to this part of the design.

6. Create the background by using smoothy squares. The finished design is 24 squares wide by 26 squares tall. Group similar colors together to produce subtle impressions of reflected light and shadows. I arranged warm pockets of color near the top of the design and cool colors near the bottom.

7. To create a shadow near the base of the bouquet, use squares with a little more texture and color than the light-value background squares. This produces a subtle shadow that does not detract from the bouquet.

I used the back side of the shadow squares along the outer edges of the shadow, and the front side in the darkest part of the shadow.

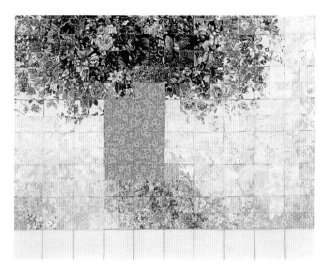

Quilt Top Assembly and Finishing

1. Sew the squares together, being careful not to mix them up as you sew. Place a pin in the top square of each vertical row when you begin sewing to help mark the top of the row. Press seams up in the odd-numbered rows; press them down in the even-numbered rows. Use a dry iron. To ensure precisely matched seams, pin each intersection before sewing the rows together. Stitch seams carefully so they are always straight, with no gentle curves. Press the entire top, using steam, so all seams lie flat.

2. From the border fabric, cut 4 strips, each 3½" x 49", cutting along the lengthwise grain.

3. Measure the quilt top through the center for mitered borders. Sew the borders to the quilt top, mitering the corners.

4. Layer the quilt top with batting and backing; baste. Quilt as desired or outline-quilt all large blossoms, tendrils, and vines for dimension. Use free-flowing curved lines or stipple quilting in the background to soften the overall image.

5. Add a hanging sleeve and a label to the back of the quilt. Bind the edges of the quilt.

SALLY SCHNEIDER

Sally grew up in northeastern Pennsylvania and has been sewing since she was a child. Her mother inspired her to learn to quilt when she gave her a pair of quilted pillows for Christmas in 1974.

Sally continued to experiment with other kinds of needlework, but quilting soon won out over everything else. She began teaching others to make quilts and eventually started writing. She is the author of *Scrap Happy: Quick-Pieced Scrap Quilts, Painless Borders,* and *ScrapMania: More Quick-Pieced Scrap Quilts.* She recently retired from teaching to become an editor at That Patchwork Place, but she still loves to make quilts, and now that her children are grown, she has more time for it.

Sally also enjoys photography and hiking in the mountains. She lives in Mill Creek, Washington, with her dog, Merlin.

Designer's Statement   For many years, I have been experimenting with the Shaded Four Patch block that uses the Mary's Triangles technique introduced in *ScrapMania.* I have developed many new designs with the block. "Time Flies!" was the result of duplicating a part of another design and rotating that part around a center. I added some pieces, changed the direction of others, and determined that fabrics in a color menu of blue and red with a tan background would best serve the design. I designed this arrangement almost ten years to the day after I first developed the Mary's Triangles technique and could hardly believe that it had been ten years. Oh, how time flies!

Sally and I share a passion for traditional quilts, especially scrap quilts. In her first book, Scrap Happy, *she found a way to utilize extra strips and scraps to make quick-pieced quilts. Sally's sunny personality makes her a joy to be around, a fact evidenced by all the friends she has made in the many places she has lived. In her recent career change to editor, Sally's twenty-five years of quiltmaking, teaching, and writing serve her well. Her co-workers recently benefited when Sally moved into a small condominium. She sorted through her fabric collection, brought unwanted fabrics and a scale to the office, and sold fabric by the pound!*

—NJM

Time Flies!
by Sally Schneider, 1995
Mill Creek, Washington
Finished Size: 59" x 59"

Materials: 44"-wide fabric

2 yds. tan print for background

¾ yd. total assorted dark prints for small triangles (12 bias strips, each 2¼" wide)

⅞ yd. total assorted blue prints for large triangles

⅝ yd. total assorted red prints for large triangles

¼ yd. total assorted other dark prints for large triangles

½ yd. red print for inner border

1⅞ yds. blue stripe for outer border cut on the lengthwise grain, or 1¼ yds. if you cut on the crosswise grain

65" x 65" piece of batting

4⅝ yds. for backing

⅝ yd. for binding

Bias Square Construction

1. **From the tan print, cut** 2 strips, each 12" x 42".
2. Open the strips to form a single layer. Stack 1 strip on top of the other, *both right sides up.*
3. Trim the fabric at a 45° angle as shown below. Cut 12 bias strips, each 2¼" wide.

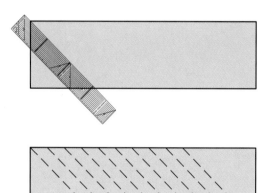

Cut 12 bias strips.

4. **From the assorted dark prints, cut** 12"-wide strips and place them on the cutting surface, *right side down.* Trim them at a 45° angle and cut 12 bias strips, each 2¼" wide.
5. Place each tan bias strip together with a dark bias strip, right sides facing. Stitch both sides of each pair, using a generous ¼"-wide seam. Press the bias strips flat to set the seams.

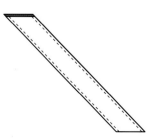

6. Place 1 bias strip unit lengthwise on your cutting table, with the long point on the left side. Line up the diagonal line of a Bias Square ruler with the left stitching line and trim away the excess fabric on the bottom.

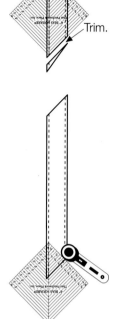

Trim.

7. Move the Bias Square so that the diagonal line is on the seam and the 2½" line is on the trimmed edge. Cut along the edge of the Bias Square.

8. Turn the bias strip over and repeat step 7. Continue to flip and cut until you have reached the end of the bias strip unit. Cut 144 bias squares. Press the seams toward the darker side and trim the "ears."

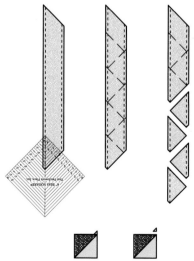

Cutting

From the background fabric, cut 9 strips, each 3½" wide, across the width of the fabric (crosswise grain). Crosscut 144 rectangles, each 2½" x 3½".

From the assorted blue, red, and other dark prints, cut 4½" x 5½" rectangles. Cut 40 blue rectangles, 24 red rectangles, and 8 dark rectangles.

Block Construction

1. Stitch each background rectangle to a bias square, positioning the dark fabric as shown below. Press the seam toward the rectangle.

Make 144.

2. Sew pairs of units together, alternating the placement of the dark triangle as shown below.

Make 72.

3. Clip the seam allowance in the center of the sewn unit. Clip completely through the stitched line. Press seams toward the rectangles.

Clip.

4. From template plastic, cut a 4½" x 4½" square. Cut the template once diagonally to make a triangle. Place the template on the wrong side of each pieced rectangle, with the corner of the template on the bias square. Draw a diagonal line across the pieced rectangle unit. Repeat on the opposite corner of the pieced rectangle. Repeat with each pieced rectangle.

Template   Drawn lines

Template

5. Place each dark rectangle together with a pieced rectangle, right sides facing. Stitch on the drawn lines and cut between them. Trim the seam allowances to ¼" wide if desired. Press the seams toward the dark triangle in each unit.

Make 144.

Quilt Top Assembly and Finishing

1. Referring to the quilt photo on page 99, arrange 5 blue, 3 red, and 1 square of assorted colors as shown below. Stitch the squares together in rows. Press seams in opposite directions from row to row. Sew the rows together. Make 16 blocks.

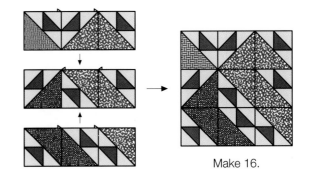

Make 16.

2. Arrange the blocks in 4 rows of 4 blocks each as shown below. Sew the blocks together in rows. Press the seams in opposite directions from row to row. Sew the rows together.

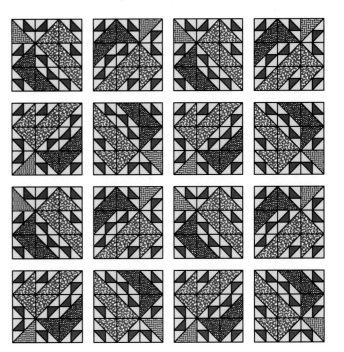

3. From the inner border fabric, cut 6 strips, each 2" x 42". Cut 2 strips in half crosswise and sew 1 piece to each of the remaining 4 border strips.

4. Measure the quilt top for straight-cut borders. Trim 2 strips to fit the sides; stitch them to the side edges of the quilt top. Press all seams toward the border.

5. Trim the 2 remaining strips to fit the top and bottom; sew to the top and bottom edges of the quilt top.

6. From the outer border fabric, cut 6 strips, each 4½" x 63". Cut on the lengthwise grain if you are using a striped fabric. (If you cut your borders on the crosswise grain, cut 8 strips and sew 4 pairs of 2 strips together to make borders that are long enough for your quilt. Measure and add the borders as shown in steps 4 and 5 at left.)

7. Measure the quilt top for borders with mitered corners. Trim 2 strips to fit the sides; stitch to the side edges of the quilt top. Trim the 2 remaining strips to fit the top and bottom; sew to the top and bottom edges of the quilt top, mitering the corners.

8. Layer the quilt top with batting and backing; baste. Quilt as desired or see the quilting suggestion below.

9. Add a hanging sleeve and a label to the back of the quilt. Bind the edges of the quilt.

In the Land of Little Quilts

SYLVIA JOHNSON,
ALICE BERG,
AND MARY ELLEN VON HOLT—
LITTLE QUILTS

Sylvia, Alice, and Mary Ellen (left to right) are longtime Quilt Market friends. As a group, we love to share decorating and photo-styling ideas. Individually, we discuss our varied interests—Alice and I talk about ideas for decorating her new house, I keep abreast of the rock music group Mary Ellen's husband belongs to, and I enjoy hearing about the kayaking and canoeing adventures Sylvia has with her family. If they ever decide to change careers, I recommend stand-up comedy. At 1995's That Patchwork Place University, Alice narrated a very entertaining presentation while Sylvia and Mary Ellen acted out the parts.

—NJM

Sylvia, Alice, and Mary Ellen are partners in the company called Little Quilts, and authors of *Little Quilts—All Through the House* and *Celebrate! with Little Quilts*. They have combined their skills, developed through years of quilting experience, in the areas of fabric choice, scale of design, techniques, and decorating with Little Quilts.

Their pattern and kit business is known worldwide for traditionally inspired doll quilts. They started it as a cottage industry, and their excitement for what they do continues to build as they combine a love for quilting with busy family and community lives. Located in the Atlanta, Georgia, area, the trio is active in local quilt activities, including the East Cobb Quilters' Guild.

Designers' Statement   When we first began our partnership as Little Quilts, we made doll-sized quilts and sold them at antique festivals in the Atlanta area. Our quilts were displayed on clotheslines and, as each buyer removed a selection from the line, we hung another Little Quilt. After several successful shows and sewing feverishly in preparation for each one, we developed the idea for kits and patterns so everyone in the world could have a Little Quilt, as it had quickly become obvious that we could not make enough!

This quilt combines our love for multi-fabric quilts with simple patchwork. We have always loved houses, so we created the perfect neighborhood—a house for each of us and one for you, with Little Quilts airing in the sun on our trademark—the ever-present clothesline.

In the Land of Little Quilts
by Little Quilts, 1995
Marietta, Georgia
Finished Size: 44" x 54"

Materials: 44"-wide fabric

Note: This is a scrap quilt and it requires small amounts of many different fabrics. We used a hand-dyed "sky" fabric for the background; substitute a solid or similar-looking fabric if you prefer.

1 yd. blue print for sky

1 yd. total assorted green prints for blocks

1 yd. total assorted brown prints for blocks

⅓ yd. total assorted light and medium blue prints for blocks

½ yd. total assorted red prints for blocks

¼ yd. total assorted light brown and tan prints for blocks

⅛ yd. total assorted purple prints for blocks

⅛ yd. total assorted gold prints for blocks

¼ yd. tan print for clothesline

4 pieces of batting in the following sizes:
    1 piece, 48" x 58"
    3 pieces, each 16" x 19"

3½ yds. backing for all quilts

⅛ yd. brown for binding background quilt

¼ yd. green for binding background quilt

The Background Quilt

Construct the background quilt first, then make the three individual Little Quilts and pin them to the background quilt. You can remove the Little Quilts and use them separately. Perhaps you would like to change quilts on the line with the changing seasons. The clothesline is a great place to showcase your work.

Cutting

Use the patterns on page 143 to make templates for the House blocks. Rotary cut the following pieces. Measurements include a ¼"-wide seam allowance.

From the sky print, cut:
    1 rectangle, 26½" x 36½", for center panel
    1 rectangle, 6½" x 8½", for house panel (Section 3)
    1 rectangle, 2½" x 8½", for house panel (Section 3)
    9 squares, each 2½" x 2½"
    4 rectangles, each 2" x 3½", for star blocks
    4 squares, each 2" x 2", for star blocks

From assorted light blue prints, including sky print, cut:
    17 squares, each 2⅞" x 2⅞". Cut the squares once diagonally for 34 triangles. There will be 1 extra.

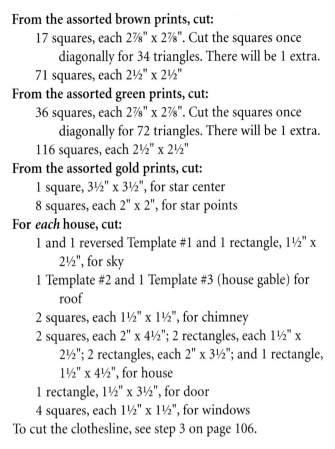

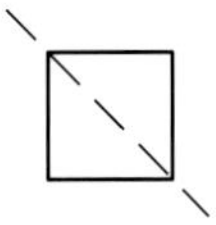

From the assorted brown prints, cut:
    17 squares, each 2⅞" x 2⅞". Cut the squares once diagonally for 34 triangles. There will be 1 extra.
    71 squares, each 2½" x 2½"

From the assorted green prints, cut:
    36 squares, each 2⅞" x 2⅞". Cut the squares once diagonally for 72 triangles. There will be 1 extra.
    116 squares, each 2½" x 2½"

From the assorted gold prints, cut:
    1 square, 3½" x 3½", for star center
    8 squares, each 2" x 2", for star points

For *each* house, cut:
    1 and 1 reversed Template #1 and 1 rectangle, 1½" x 2½", for sky
    1 Template #2 and 1 Template #3 (house gable) for roof
    2 squares, each 1½" x 1½", for chimney
    2 squares, each 2" x 4½"; 2 rectangles, each 1½" x 2½"; 2 rectangles, each 2" x 3½"; and 1 rectangle, 1½" x 4½", for house
    1 rectangle, 1½" x 3½", for door
    4 squares, each 1½" x 1½", for windows

To cut the clothesline, see step 3 on page 106.

Block Construction

1. To make the star block, draw a diagonal line from corner to corner on the wrong side of each 2" x 2" star-point square. Place 1 square on the end of a 2" x 3½" sky rectangle. Sew on the marked line. Trim the corner of the triangle, leaving a narrow seam allowance. *Do not trim the rectangle corner.* Press the triangle toward the corner. Place a second square on the other end of the rectangle, with the marked line crossing the previous seam. Sew, trim, and press. Make 4 units.

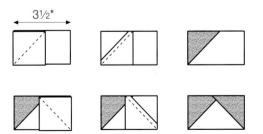

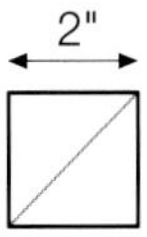

Make 4.

2. Arrange the star points with the 3½" square of gold fabric and the 2" squares of sky fabric. Sew the pieces together in rows and press as shown. Sew the rows together to make 1 star.

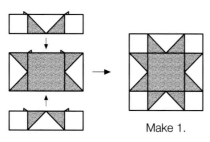

Make 1.

3. From tan print for the clothesline, cut enough 1¼"-wide bias strips to make a strip approximately 38" long. Sew the bias strips together; fold and press them into thirds.

Appliqué the strip to the large sky piece, placing the left end about 5½" down from the top, and the right end about 4½" down from the top. Trim away the excess clothesline.

4. Arrange the pieces for 1 House block and sew them together, following the diagrams below. Press seams as shown. Make 4 House blocks.

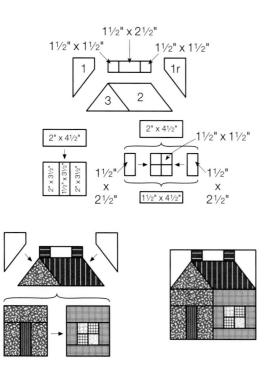

5. Sew 34 green triangles to 34 sky triangles. Press these seams and all remaining seams toward the darker fabric in each resulting half-square triangle unit. Sew 7 green triangles to 7 brown triangles. Sew 34 green triangles together in pairs to make 17 squares. Sew 26 brown triangles together in pairs to make 13 squares.

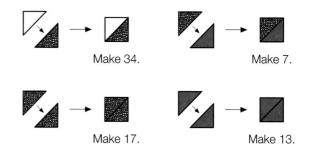

Make 34.   Make 7.

Make 17.   Make 13.

6. Arrange the star block with the squares and pieced squares as shown below for Section 1. Refer to the color photo on page 104. Sew the pieces together in rows and press the seams in opposite directions from row to row. Sew the rows together.

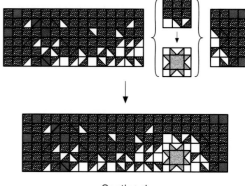

Section 1

7. Arrange the clothesline/sky panel with the appropriate squares and pieced squares for Section 2. Sew the pieces together in rows and press the seams toward the panel. Sew the rows together.

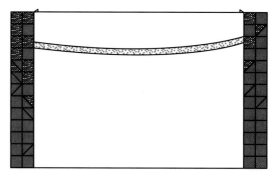

Section 2

8. Arrange 1 House block with the 2½" x 8½" sky rectangle, squares, and pieced squares for Unit A. Sew the pieces together in rows and press; sew the rows together.

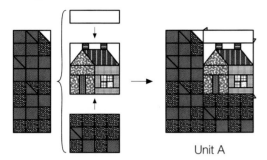

Unit A

9. Arrange 1 House block with the appropriate squares and pieced squares for Unit B. Sew the pieces together in rows and press; sew the rows together.

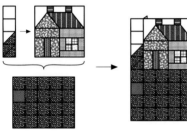

Unit B

10. Arrange 1 House block with the appropriate squares and 6½" x 8½" sky rectangle for Unit C. Sew the pieces together in rows; press. Sew the rows together.

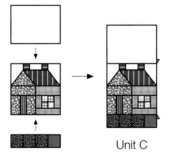

Unit C

11. Arrange 1 House block with the appropriate squares and pieced squares for Unit D. Sew the pieces together in rows and press; sew the rows together.

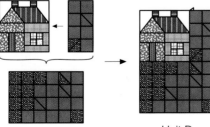

Unit D

12. Sew the units together to complete Section 3.

Section 3

Quilt Top Assembly and Finishing

1. Arrange the sections as shown and sew together.

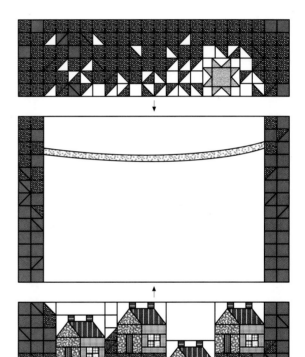

2. Layer the quilt top with batting and backing; baste. Quilt as desired or see the quilting suggestion below.

3. Add a hanging sleeve and a label to the back.
4. Cut straight-grain strips for single-layer binding as follows and sew them together in the order listed:

    1 brown strip, 1¼" x 42"
    Green strips to measure 1¼" x 55"
    1 brown strip, 1¼" x 26"
    Green strips to measure 1¼" x 80"

5. Beginning on the right side of the quilt near the clothesline, sew the binding around the quilt, mitering the corners. The binding colors do not intersect the blocks exactly at the seams; they blend as they go around the quilt.
6. Construct the Little Quilts on the following pages and hang them on the clothesline. We pinned them to the quilt from the back and added tiny clothespins.

The Little Quilts

Make each of these quilts individually. Use very thin batting (we suggest cotton), and tea dye or gently wash them to soften the look. Press.

Heart and Nine Patch

Finished Size: 12" x 15"

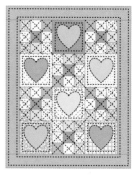

1. From the assorted tan prints, cut 6 squares, each 3½" x 3½", for the Heart blocks. From the assorted red prints, cut 6 hearts using the pattern on page 143. Add ¼"-wide seam allowances around each heart.
2. Appliqué each heart to a background square.
3. From assorted fabrics, cut 18 strips, each 1½" x 6". Sew the strips together in groups of 3; press the seams to one side. Cut 18 segments, each 1½" wide, from the strip sets. Join groups of 3 segments to make 6 Nine Patch blocks.

For random-color Nine Patch blocks:

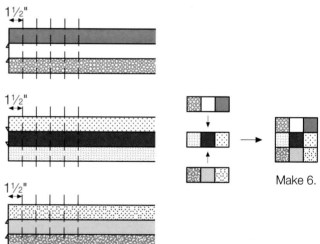

Make 6.

4. Arrange the blocks as shown in the quilt plan above. Sew the blocks together in rows; press seams in opposite directions from row to row. Sew the rows together.
5. From the border fabric, cut 2 strips, each 1¾" x 12½". Sew them to the side edges of the quilt top. Cut 2 strips, each 1¾" x 12", and sew them to the top and bottom edges of the quilt top.
6. Layer the quilt top with backing and thin batting; baste. Referring to the quilt plan above, quilt around each heart and ¼" inside the outer edges of each background block. Crosshatch the Nine Patch blocks. Quilt the border with straight lines spaced ¼", then ¾" from the seam line.
7. Bind the edges with 1¼"-wide straight-grain strips.

Scrappy Stars Quilt

Finished Size: 11½" x 15½"

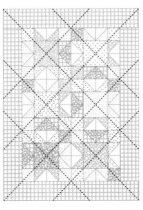

1. From assorted fabrics, cut 6 squares, each 2½" x 2½", for the star centers. Cut 24 squares, each 1⅞" x 1⅞"; cut them once diagonally for 48 triangles for the star points. Cut 24 squares, each 1⅞" x 1⅞"; cut them once diagonally for 48 triangles for the background. Cut 24 squares, each 1½" x 1½", for the corners of the star blocks.

2. Sew each star-point triangle to a star-background triangle as shown below. Press the seams toward the darker fabric in each square.

3. Arrange 8 star points, 4 background corner squares, and 1 center square as shown; sew them together to make 1 star block. Press seams as shown below. Repeat to make 6 star blocks.

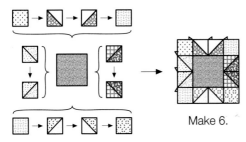

Make 6.

4. Arrange the blocks as shown in the quilt plan above. Sew them together in rows; press seams in opposite directions from row to row. Sew rows together.

5. From the border fabric, cut 2 strips, each 2" x 12½", and sew them to opposite side edges of the quilt top. Cut 2 strips, each 2" x 11½", and sew them to the top and bottom edges of the quilt top.

6. Layer the quilt top with batting and backing; baste. Quilt as desired or as shown in the quilt plan above.

7. Bind the edges with 1¼"-wide straight-grain strips.

Log Cabin Quilt

Finished Size: 9¼" x 12⅜"

1. From assorted fabrics, cut 1⅛"-wide strips of both dark and light fabric. Cut 6 red squares, each 1⅛" x 1⅛", for the block centers.

2. Select a light strip and sew it to a red center square. Trim the strip even with the center square; press the seam and all remaining seams *away* from the center square.

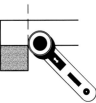

3. With the right side up, turn the block so that the last sewn strip is at the top. Add a second light strip as shown. Add 2 dark strips in the same manner.

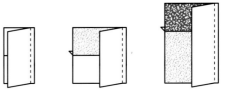

4. Continue adding light and dark strips until the block has 2 rounds of dark and 2 rounds of light.

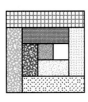

Make 6.

5. Repeat steps 2–4 to make a total of 6 blocks.

6. Arrange the blocks as shown in the quilt plan above. Sew them together in rows; press seams in opposite directions from row to row. Sew rows together.

7. From the border fabric, cut 2 strips, each 1¾" x 9⅞", and sew them to opposite side edges of the quilt top. Cut 2 strips, each 1¾" x 9¼", and sew them to the top and bottom edges of the quilt top. Press the seams toward the border.

8. Layer the quilt top with batting and backing; baste. Quilt as desired or as shown in the quilt plan above.

9. Bind the edges with 1¼"-wide straight-grain strips.

I have long admired Christal's Log Cabin quilts, so I wrote to her in 1986 asking if she would combine her most popular patterns into a book. The result was Holiday Happenings. *My favorite story about Christal concerns the night she quickly jumped into bed after an evening of quilting. She thought her quilting needle may have become imbedded in her arm, but she couldn't see it. Her husband, Bill, went to his workshop, produced his stud finder, and confirmed that Christal's quilting needle was indeed imbedded deep beneath her skin. He took the stud finder along to the emergency room to help the doctor locate the missing needle.*

—NJM

Circle of Friends

CHRISTAL CARTER

Christal is recognized for her pictorial quilts and Log Cabin picture quilts with appliquéd details. Many of her quilts have won prizes, and her work has taken her throughout the United States and to Canada and Australia to teach. She offers a variety of classes and lectures on quilts and decorating. She is also the author of three successful books featuring her quilt designs, *Holiday Happenings, Quilts for All Seasons—Year-Round Log Cabin Designs,* and *A Child's Garden of Quilts.*

Christal owns and operates Majestic Seasons, decorators for hotel and corporate theme parties and seasonal events. She makes her home in Southern California with her husband, Bill.

Designer's Statement   It is because of the many friends I have made at That Patchwork Place that I decided to design "Circle of Friends." Using my favorite block, the Log Cabin, I made off-center diamond blocks to form the six "friends." I love appliqué and embroidery, so detailing the gowns and faces was fun. I hope each of the quilters who makes this pattern will enjoy personalizing the quilt with her own family and circle of friends.

Circle of Friends
by Christal Carter, 1995
Valley Center, California
Finished Size: 40" x 46"

Materials: 44"-wide fabric

1¼ yds. small-scale floral print for center garden area and
    binding
¼ yd. each of 4 similar aqua prints for sky
⅛ yd. each of 3 different yellow prints for gowns
⅛ yd. each of 3 different pink prints for gowns
⅔ yd. large-scale floral print for border
Assorted scraps of various skin tones for hands and faces
44" x 50" piece of batting
1½ yds. for backing
Embroidery floss: black, white, and pink, plus different
    colors for hair
Assorted scraps of lace and ribbon for gown and hat trim
4mm silk embroidery ribbon for garland
Ribbon roses for garland and hats (optional)
Acrylic 60° to 120° diamond template*

*These angles are often found on large rotary-cutting
rulers and will work, but it is easier if you have a precut
diamond template. Any size will do as long as the angles
are correct. Or, you may make your own template from
the large diamond pattern on page 129.

Cutting

From the small-scale floral print, cut a 16" x 24" rect-
    angle and reserve it for the binding.
From each of the 4 aqua fabrics, cut 4 strips, each
    1½" x 42". Reserve 6 assorted aqua strips for borders.
From each yellow and pink gown print, cut 2 strips, each
    1½" x 42".
From the small-scale floral print, cut 15 strips, each
    1½" x 42".
    Make a plastic template for the small diamonds,
using the pattern on page 129.

Block Construction

1. Using the small diamond template, cut 6 diamonds
   from 1 of the aqua fabric strips, 1 for the center of
   each block.
2. Lay a strip of small-scale floral print right side up on
   the sewing machine. Place the aqua diamonds wrong
   side up on the strip in the direction shown in the
   illustration above right, and stitch ¼" from the right
   edge. Press the seam allowance toward the floral strip.

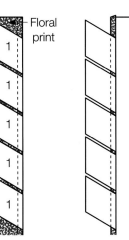

Floral print

Place diamonds
with the upper tips
pointing to the left.

Press seams
toward the
fabric strip.

3. Place the large diamond template on the first diamond as shown, keeping the edges of the template
   even with the raw edges of the strip and the diamond. The 120° angle should be at the top. Cut the
   double-diamond units apart and trim away any
   excess fabric between the blocks.

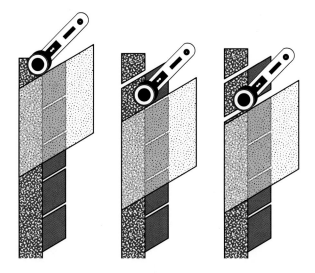

4. Lay another strip of the small-scale
   floral print right side up on the
   machine. Place the blocks *wrong
   side up* on the strip as shown. Keep
   the most recently added fabric
   nearest you as you place it on the
   machine. Place the top edge of the
   block 1½" away from the top edge
   of the strip to allow enough fabric
   for the angled cutting.

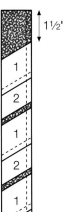

1½"

Tip:

~ When the left edge of the block angles upward, leave 1½" extra at the bottom of the strip for the angled cutting.

~ When the left edge of the block angles downward, leave 1½" extra at the top of the strip for the angled cutting.

~ Always place the block on the strip so that the piece you added last is toward you.

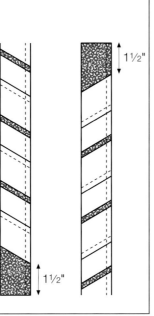

8. To construct the gown blocks, cut 1 small diamond from each of the 3 yellow and 3 pink prints. Place the diamonds on a strip of small-scale floral print as shown. Stitch, press, and cut apart.

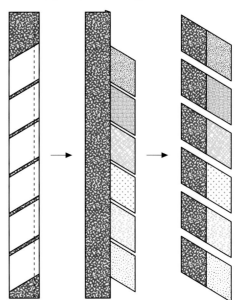

5. Press seams toward the fabric strip. Cut the blocks apart using the large diamond template to keep angles accurate.

6. Choose a different aqua print and lay the strip on the machine. Place the blocks on the strip as shown with the most recently added fabric nearest you. Stitch the blocks to the strip; press and cut them apart using the large diamond template to keep the angles accurate.

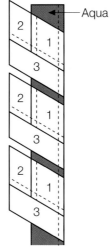

7. Continue this piecing sequence, mixing the aqua fabrics randomly, through piece #13. Reserve the diamond blocks for steps 5–7 on page 114. You will add the sleeves to complete the blocks at that time.

9. Continue adding strips as you did for the 6 background blocks to complete the blocks. Use gown fabric in positions 1, 4, 5, 8, 9, 12, and 13. Make 1 block with each gown print for a total of 6 blocks.

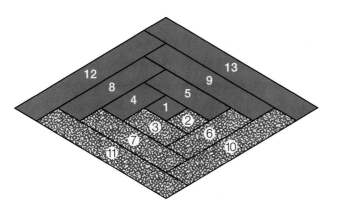

Make 1 block with each gown fabric.

Quilt Top Assembly

1. Arrange the 6 gown blocks together to form a star, alternating the pink and yellow, and keeping the small-scale floral print in the center.

2. Sew 2 diamonds together (1 with pink and 1 with yellow), stopping the stitching ¼" away from the wide point of the diamonds. Repeat to make 2 diamond-pair units.

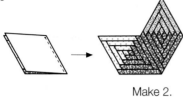

Make 2.

3. Sew 1 diamond to each of the 2 diamond-pair units, making sure that the gown fabrics alternate.

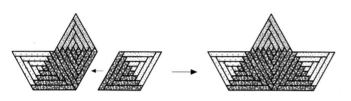

4. Sew the 2 units together, matching the centers.

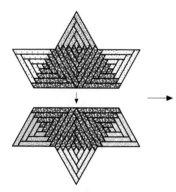

Note: To match centers, place a pin through the intersection of the two seams of the center diamond. Push it through the intersection of the seams of the opposite diamond. Pull the pin snug, then pin through the seam allowance on either side of the center pin. Remove the center pin and sew the seam. Be sure the needle goes directly through the intersection of the diamonds.

5. To complete the remaining blocks and make sleeves for the gown, cut 2 strips, each 1½" x 4", from each gown print. Sew each sleeve to a 1½" x 8" aqua strip as shown.

Pink or yellow fabric	Aqua

6. Arrange the incomplete blocks between the gowns to determine which arm units must be added to each block. Each diamond block requires 1 pink and 1 yellow sleeve section.

7. Pin the seam of the left sleeve unit exactly 3" from the tip of the block. There will be excess fabric at each end. Stitch the strip to the block; press and trim the excess fabric. Add the right sleeve unit in the same manner.

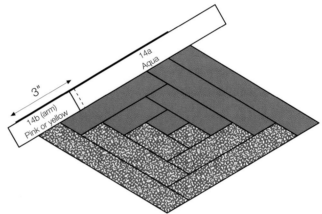

Pin arm seam 3" from diamond point.

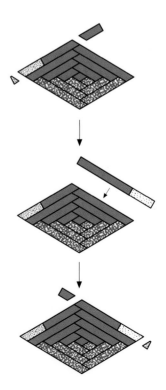

8. Arrange the completed background diamond blocks so that the gown sleeves are in the right places. Sew each diamond into the star, making a hexagonal unit.

9. Sew 2 rows of aqua strips around the hexagon shape, following the numerical order from 1–12 as shown below. Use the large diamond template to trim each strip so that the 120° angle is correct.

10. From the large-scale floral, cut 5 strips, each 4" x 42". Cut 1 strip in half crosswise. Sew borders to the quilt in numerical order as shown above, using the 2 short strips for #13 and #14 and trimming excess fabric as you go.

Finishing

1. Using the patterns on page 128, cut out the faces and hands from the skin-colored fabrics. Use different skin tones to represent your own friends and relatives. Cut 6 hats from appropriate fabrics. Add ¼" seam allowances around each piece when cutting. Referring to the quilt photo on page 111, appliqué heads, hands, and hats.

2. Embroider faces as shown on the appliqué pattern. Embellish the hats and gowns using scraps of lace and ribbon.

3. Connect each lady to the next with a silk ribbon garland. Attach the garland with French knots or appliqué it in place. Embellish with ribbon roses after quilting is completed.

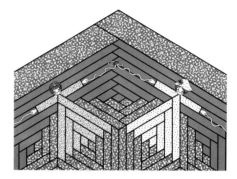

4. Layer the quilt top with batting and backing; baste. Quilt as desired or see the quilting suggestion below.

5. Add a hanging sleeve and a label to the back of the quilt. From the reserved rectangle of small floral fabric, cut 6 strips, each 2½" x 24". Bind one edge at a time, folding over the raw edges and tucking them in.

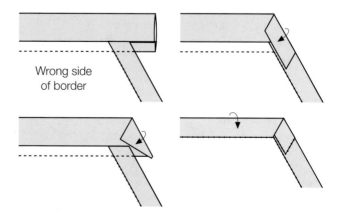

Wrong side of border

Jackstripe

DONNA LYNN THOMAS

Born and raised in southeastern Pennsylvania, Donna started sewing when she was four years old. Since her mother was a home-economics teacher and her father an engineer, it seems only natural that Donna—with a love of fabric and stitching, and a passion for geometry and math—would take to quilting.

Donna has been quilting since 1975 and teaching since 1982. She earned her National Quilting Association teacher's certification in 1988. The introduction of rotary-cutting tools in the early 1980s revolutionized her approach to quiltmaking. Since that time, she has worked exclusively on rotary-cut and machine-pieced quilts, focusing on applications of bias strip piecing.

She is the author of five books: *Small Talk*, *Shortcuts: A Concise Guide to Rotary Cutting*, *A Perfect Match: A Guide to Precise Machine Piecing*, *Shortcuts to the Top*, and *Stripples*. The metric version of *Shortcuts* has been translated into four languages, and *Shortcuts to the Top* was also issued in German by a German publisher. Donna is a contributing author to *The Quilters' Companion: Everything You Need to Know to Make Beautiful Quilts*. In addition, she has designed a new ruler, the Bias Stripper™, to make it possible to cut accurate, properly sized bias strips without any complicated math.

The Thomas family consists of Donna, her husband, Terry (whose hobby is cooking), and their two teenage sons, Joseph and Peter. Terry's military career has taken them many places and, as a result, Donna has had the opportunity to teach quiltmaking in many parts of the country as well as overseas. They recently moved from Kansas to Georgia, where Donna continues to make quilts, write, teach, and pursue her other passion—gardening.

I first met Donna in 1987 while she was teaching at Patch of Country in Chadds Ford, Pennsylvania. She was then paring down her fabric collection as she prepared for a military relocation to Germany. Donna was certain that making miniature quilts would be a good solution. Working in miniature helped Donna refine her piecing skills and think about the basics of rotary cutting, which she turned into the best-selling, rotary-cutting reference book, Shortcuts. *She has since written four additional books, most recently* Stripples—*her ever-fertile mind came up with a new strip-piecing technique and a ruler to accompany it!*

—NJM

Designer's Statement   "Jackstripe" is a rotary-cut, machine-pieced quilt that combines some of my favorite aspects of quilt-making—small blocks and bias strip piecing. I've been fascinated with bias strip piecing ever since I learned how to make bias squares from Nancy Martin in 1987. Since then, I've been applying the concept to eliminate steps and improve accuracy in all types of pieced squares, triangles, and rectangles constructed with bias seams.

"Jackstripe" is built two blocks at a time from trios of prints, enabling you to make the quilt as small or large as you wish, using small amounts of fabric. You won't have to do any extra figuring for fabric yardage to make a larger quilt (other than borders), and you can even justify taking years to complete the quilt—two blocks at a time! The result is a scrap-look quilt made easily from trios of coordinated prints. Border fabric requirements are given for the quilt in the photo, but you may ignore them and border your quilt later based on its completed size.

If you're ready to try something different, here's a quilt to take you beyond the basics of rotary cutting and bias strip piecing. Enjoy!

Jackstripe
by Donna Lynn Thomas, 1995
Peachtree City, Georgia
Finished Size: 41" x 41"
Quilted by Kari Lane.

Materials: 44"-wide fabric

- 9" x 20" piece each of 13 teal prints
- 9" x 20" piece each of 13 cinnamon prints
- 9" x 20" piece each of 13 light prints
- ¼ yd. teal print for inner border
- ¼ yd. tan print for middle border
- ⅝ yd. multicolored print for outer border
- 49" x 49" piece of batting
- 1¼ yds. for backing
- ⅜ yd. for binding

Note: The following cutting and sewing instructions will make 2 blocks. Repeat the instructions to make additional blocks as required for your quilt.

Cutting

From 1 teal print, cut:
   1 piece, 6½" x 14½"
   1 square, 2½" x 2½"
From 1 cinnamon print, cut:
   1 piece, 6½" x 13¾"
   1 square, 2½" x 2½"
From 1 light print, cut:
   1 piece, 6½" x 13¼"

Bias Strip Piecing

1. To establish the correct angle for the bias cuts, measure 6½" along the lower left edge of the fabric, right side up, and make a mark. If you are left-handed, measure 6½" from the lower right edge, right side down. Cut from the mark to the upper corner as shown.

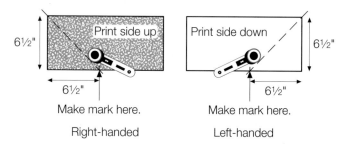

Make mark here.

Right-handed

Make mark here.

Left-handed

2. With all fabrics right side up, cut the 6½"-wide pieces into bias strips. (If you are left-handed, cut all fabrics right side down.) If you are using the Bias Stripper, use the cutting mark given in parentheses, not the strip width. Reserve both corner triangles of each fabric for step 6 on page 119.

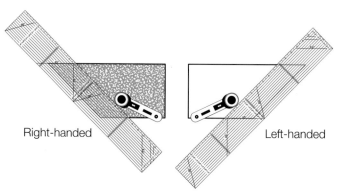

Right-handed   Left-handed

Cut bias strips starting from the bias cut.

From 1 teal print, cut:
   2 bias strips, each 1¾" wide (1¾ mark)
   2 bias strips, each 1" wide (⅝ mark)
From 1 cinnamon print, cut:
   2 bias strips, each 2½" wide (2¾ mark)
From 1 light print, cut:
   1 bias strip, 2½" wide (2¾ mark)
   2 bias strips, each 1" wide (⅝ mark)

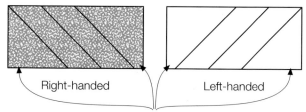

Right-handed   Left-handed

Reserve corner triangles.

3. Lay the bias strips out in the order shown below for Strip Unit 1.

Strip Unit 1 Layout
Wider teal strips are on outer edges of Strip Unit 1.

Note: Accurate ¼"-wide seam allowances are crucial to the success of this quilt. The fact that your seam allowance is consistently too small or too large is of no benefit at all. Your quilt will not go together properly if your seam allowance is not accurate. There is no substitute for accurate stitching.

4. Sew the strips together using an accurate ¼"-wide seam. Offset the strips when sewing. Begin stitching at the V, where the angled edges of the 2 strips intersect at the ¼"-wide seam allowance. This yields a

strip unit that is even along the top edge, making it easy to cut it into squares and rectangles. Always sew strips from the top of the strip unit to the bottom so that the top edge of the strip unit is even. The bottom edge will probably be uneven. Press each seam as shown before adding another strip to the strip unit. When you are working with bias strips, it is difficult to press all the seams at once on a completed strip unit and still keep the unit straight.

Offset strips so ¼" seam starts at V.

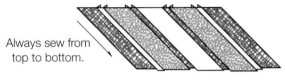

Always sew from top to bottom.

Strip Unit 1

5. Position Strip Unit 1 with the top (even) edge toward you. Tilt it as much as necessary to cut comfortably. To cut 2½" striped squares, center the diagonal line of the Bias Square ruler on the center seam line of the first striped square. Keep the 2½" dimension inside the bottom raw edge. Cut the top and left edges of the square. Pull it away from the strip unit, turn it, and trim the 2 remaining raw edges. Cut 4 Type A and 4 Type B striped squares.

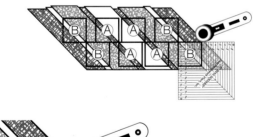

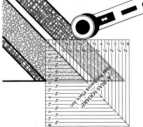

Cut top and left sides.

Turn and trim remaining 2 sides.

Type A   Type B
Cut 4.   Cut 4.

6. From each of the 2 teal, 2 cinnamon, and 2 light 6½" corner triangles, cut a bias strip 2¾" wide (3 mark on the Bias Stripper) for a total of 6 bias strips.

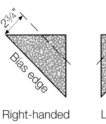

Right-handed   Left-handed

7. Sew the bias strips into pairs; press the seams as shown. Sew the bias-strip pairs into the order shown in the diagram to make Strip Unit 2. Press seams in the direction of the arrows.

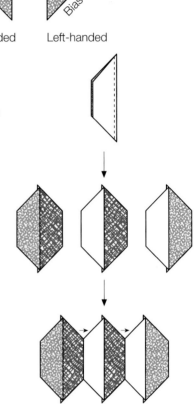

Strip Unit 2

8. Cut 8 bias squares, each 2⅞" x 2⅞", from Strip Unit 2 as shown. Lay the diagonal line of the Bias Square over the lower right or left point of the strip unit. Keep the 2⅞" marks inside the raw edge and cut the top 2 edges of the bias square from edge to edge. Turn the bias square and trim the remaining 2 raw edges to 2⅞".

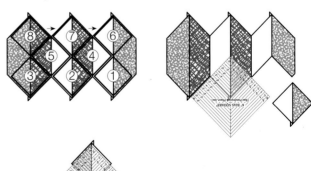

Turn and trim remaining 2 raw edges to 2⅞".

9. Continue cutting across the strip unit, moving from the lowest point to the lowest point, until all 8 bias squares are cut. You should have 2 teal/cinnamon bias squares, 4 teal/light bias squares, and 2 cinnamon/light bias squares.

Make 2.   Make 4.   Make 2.

10. Cut all 8 bias squares once diagonally to make 4 teal/cinnamon side-by-side triangles, 8 teal/light side-by-side triangles, and 4 cinnamon/light side-by-side triangles.

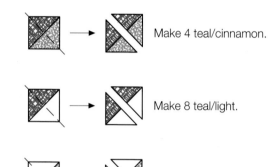

Make 4 teal/cinnamon.

Make 8 teal/light.

Make 4 cinnamon/light.

Block Construction

1. Using the side-by-side triangles, make Type A and Type B quarter-square triangle units as shown. Press all seams toward the teal/light side-by-side triangles.

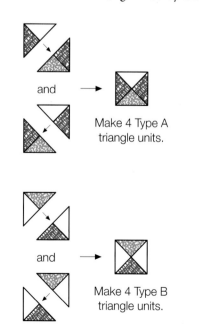

and → Make 4 Type A triangle units.

and → Make 4 Type B triangle units.

2. Arrange the 4 Type A striped squares, the 4 Type A quarter-square triangle units, and the teal 2½" square as shown below. Sew them together in rows, then sew the rows together to make 1 Jackstripe Block A. Press seams as shown.

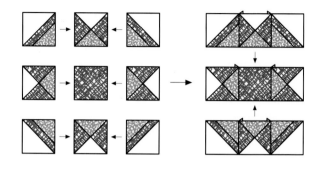

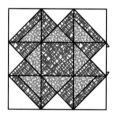

Jackstripe Block A
Make 1 from each fabric trio.

3. Arrange the 4 Type B striped squares, the 4 Type B quarter-square triangle units, and the cinnamon 2½" square to make 1 Jackstripe Block B. Stitch it together as you did Block A in step 2. Press seams as shown.

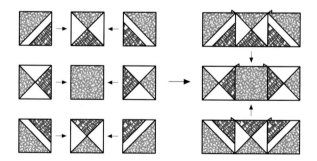

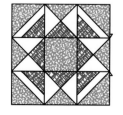

Jackstripe Block B
Make 1 from each fabric trio.

4. Repeat the same process to make as many pairs of blocks as you need for the size quilt you desire. I made 26 blocks (13 fabric trios) and used 12 Jackstripe Block A's and 13 Jackstripe Block B's for the sample quilt.

Quilt Top Assembly and Finishing

1. Arrange the 13 Block A's and 12 Block B's into 5 rows of 5 blocks each. Balance the prints and contrasts of the blocks until the layout suits you. Sew the blocks into rows, matching the seams as you stitch. Press seams in opposite directions from row to row. Sew the rows together.

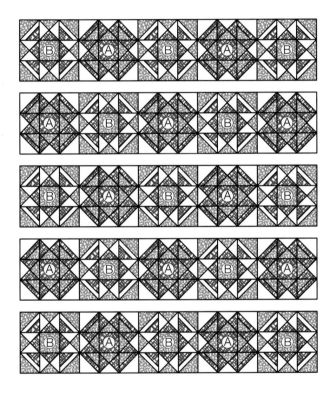

2. Cut the border and binding strips as follows:
   From the teal print for the inner border, cut:
       4 strips, each 1" x 42"
   From the tan print for the middle border, cut:
       4 strips, each 1¾" x 42"
   From the multicolored outer border print, cut:
       4 strips, each 4¼" x 42"
   From the fabric for binding, cut:
       5 strips, each 2" x 42"

3. Measure the quilt top for straight-cut borders. Trim 2 teal print strips to fit the sides; sew to the side edges of the quilt top. Press these and all remaining seams toward the border. Trim the remaining 2 strips to fit

the top and bottom; sew to the top and bottom edges of the quilt top. Repeat for the tan 1¾"-wide middle border and the 4¼"-wide multicolored outer border.

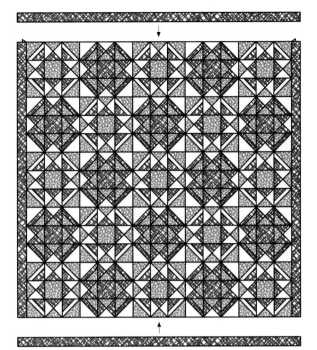

4. Layer the quilt top with batting and backing; baste. Quilt as desired or see the quilting suggestion below.

5. Add a hanging sleeve and a label to the back of the quilt. Bind the edges of the quilt.

Templates

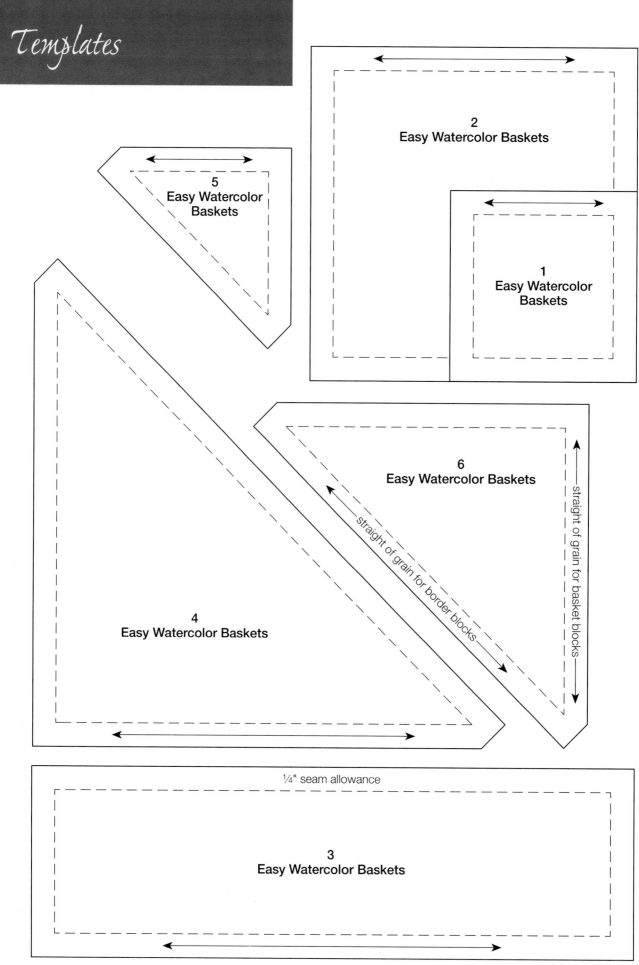

2
Easy Watercolor Baskets

5
Easy Watercolor Baskets

1
Easy Watercolor Baskets

6
Easy Watercolor Baskets

straight of grain for border blocks

straight of grain for basket blocks

4
Easy Watercolor Baskets

¼" seam allowance

3
Easy Watercolor Baskets

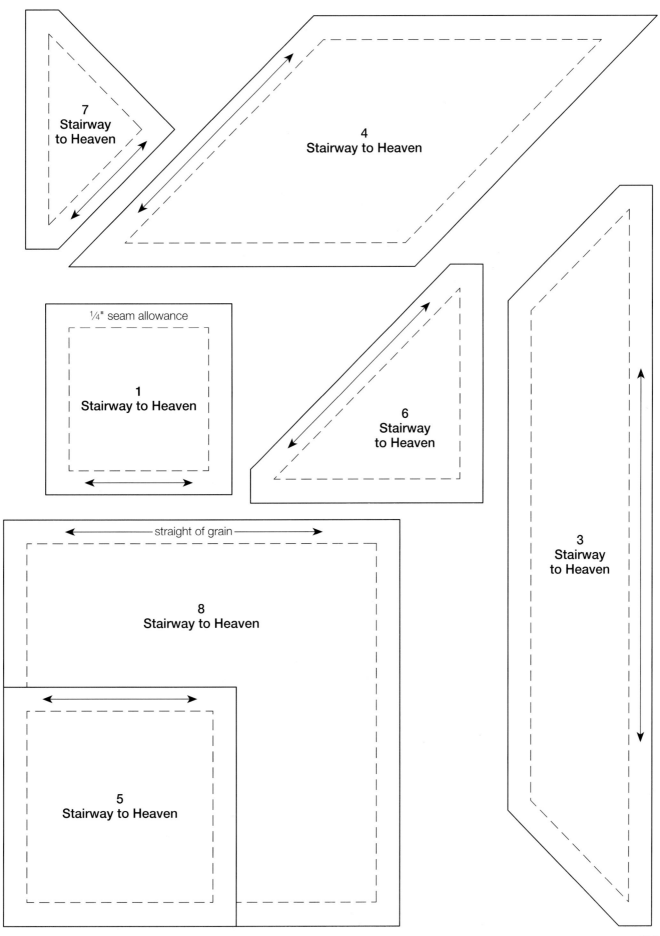

7
Stairway
to Heaven

4
Stairway to Heaven

¼" seam allowance

1
Stairway to Heaven

6
Stairway
to Heaven

3
Stairway
to Heaven

straight of grain

8
Stairway to Heaven

5
Stairway to Heaven

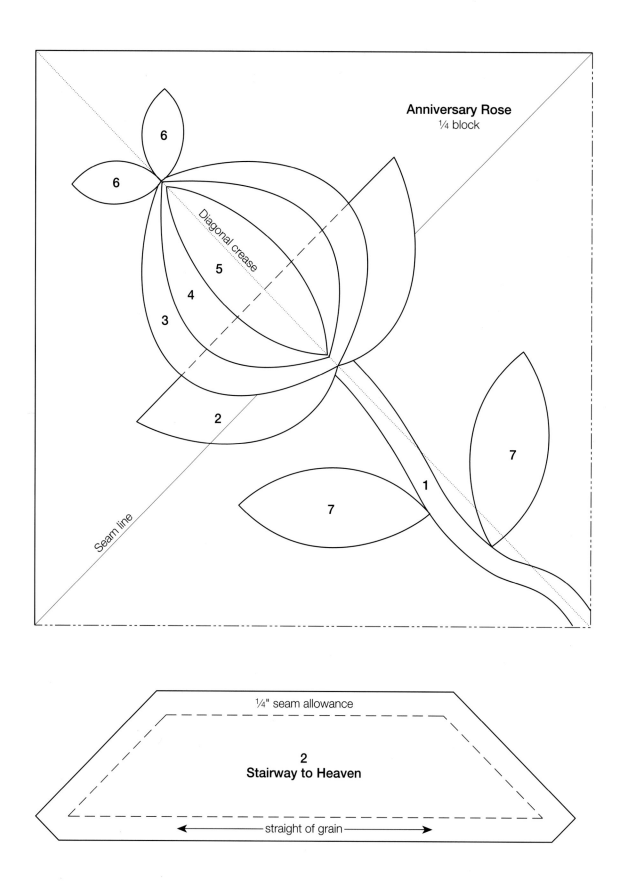

Anniversary Rose
¼ block

6

6

6

Diagonal crease

5

4

3

Seam line

2

7

1

7

¼" seam allowance

**2
Stairway to Heaven**

←——— straight of grain ———→

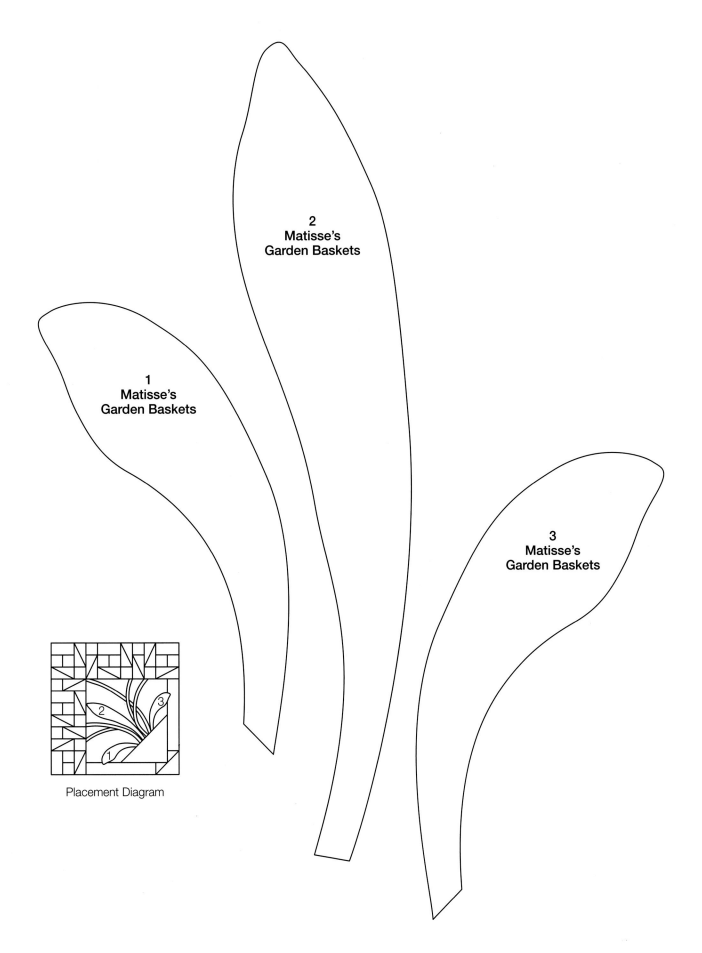

1
Matisse's
Garden Baskets

2
Matisse's
Garden Baskets

3
Matisse's
Garden Baskets

Placement Diagram

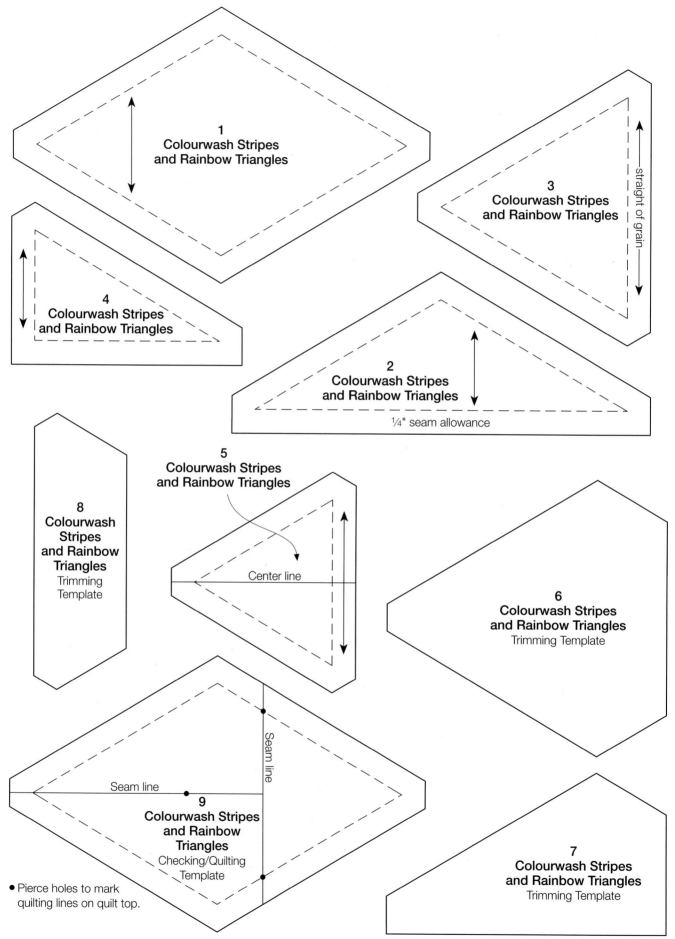

1
Colourwash Stripes
and Rainbow Triangles

3
Colourwash Stripes
and Rainbow Triangles

straight of grain

4
Colourwash Stripes
and Rainbow Triangles

2
Colourwash Stripes
and Rainbow Triangles

¼" seam allowance

5
Colourwash Stripes
and Rainbow Triangles

Center line

8
Colourwash
Stripes
and Rainbow
Triangles
Trimming
Template

6
Colourwash Stripes
and Rainbow Triangles
Trimming Template

Seam line

Seam line

9
Colourwash Stripes
and Rainbow Triangles
Checking/Quilting
Template

7
Colourwash Stripes
and Rainbow Triangles
Trimming Template

● Pierce holes to mark
quilting lines on quilt top.

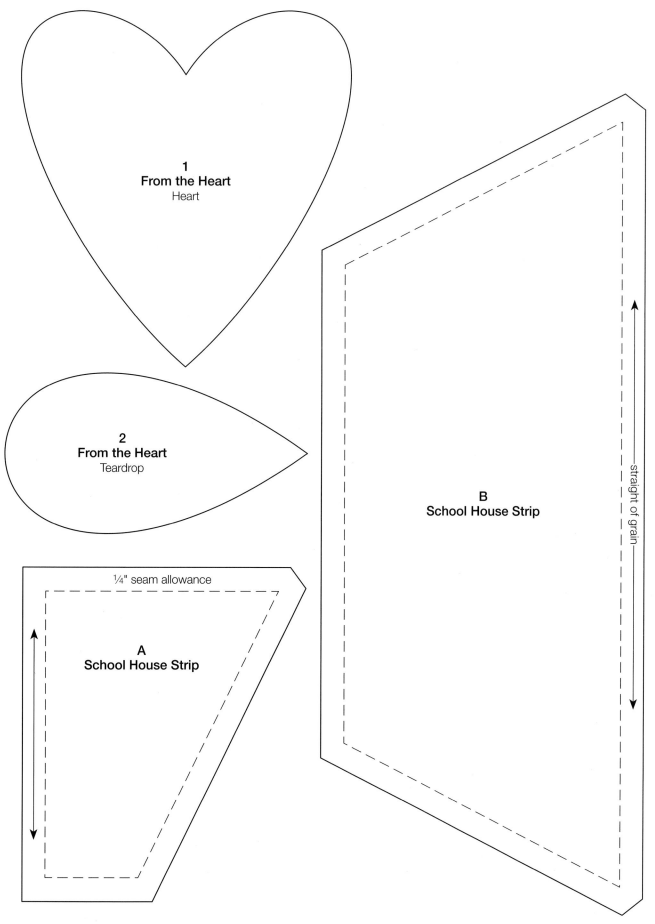

1
From the Heart
Heart

2
From the Heart
Teardrop

¼" seam allowance

A
School House Strip

B
School House Strip

straight of grain

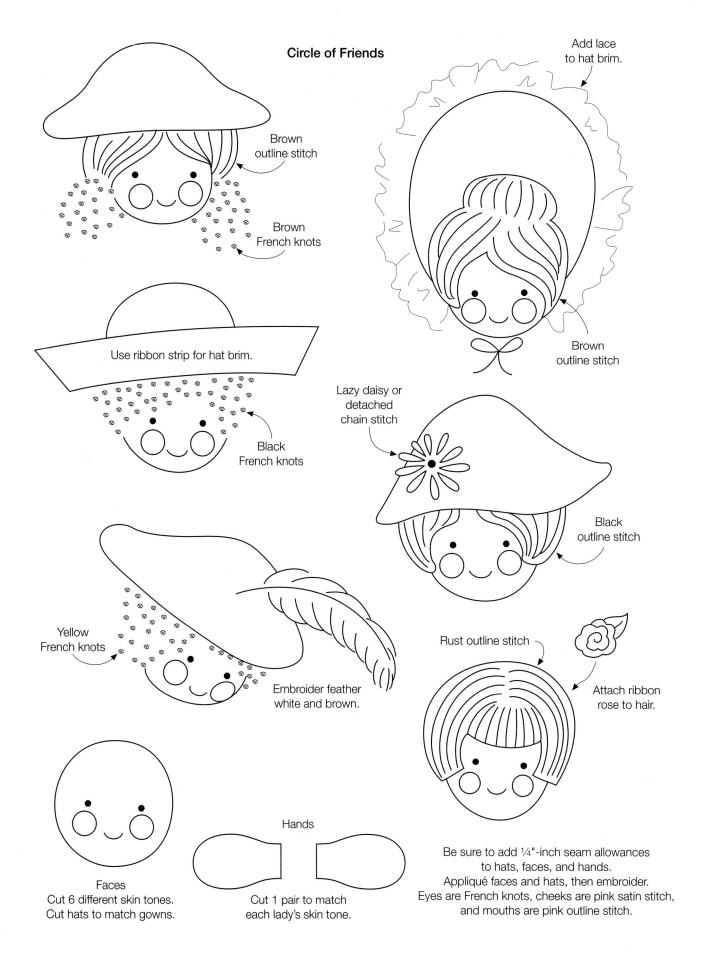

Circle of Friends

Add lace to hat brim.

Brown outline stitch

Brown French knots

Brown outline stitch

Use ribbon strip for hat brim.

Black French knots

Lazy daisy or detached chain stitch

Black outline stitch

Yellow French knots

Embroider feather white and brown.

Rust outline stitch

Attach ribbon rose to hair.

Faces
Cut 6 different skin tones.
Cut hats to match gowns.

Hands
Cut 1 pair to match each lady's skin tone.

Be sure to add ¼"-inch seam allowances to hats, faces, and hands.
Appliqué faces and hats, then embroider.
Eyes are French knots, cheeks are pink satin stitch, and mouths are pink outline stitch.

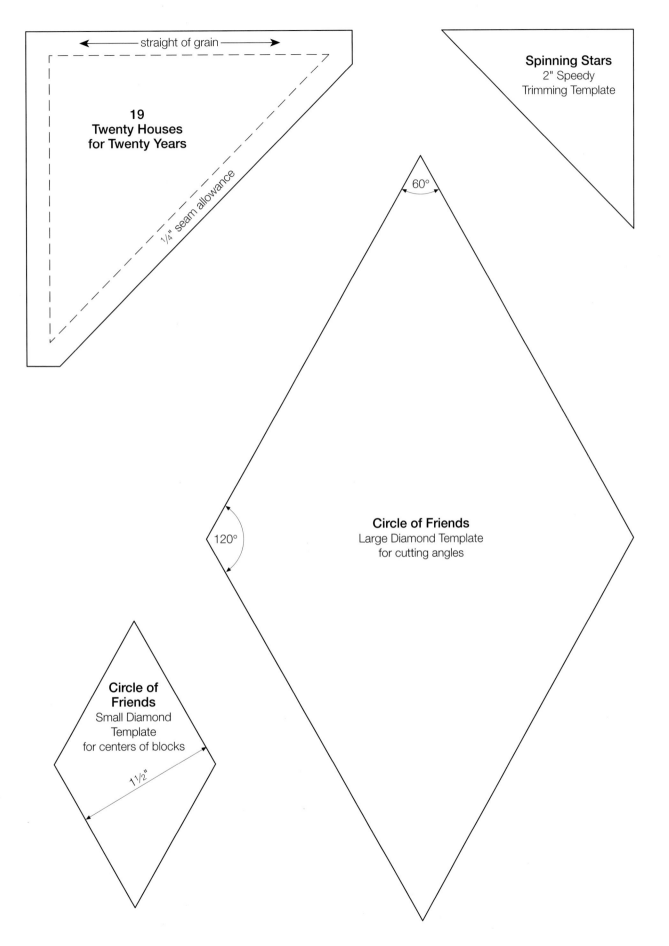

straight of grain

**19
Twenty Houses
for Twenty Years**

¼" seam allowance

Spinning Stars
2" Speedy
Trimming Template

60°

120°

Circle of Friends
Large Diamond Template
for cutting angles

**Circle of
Friends**
Small Diamond
Template
for centers of blocks

1½"

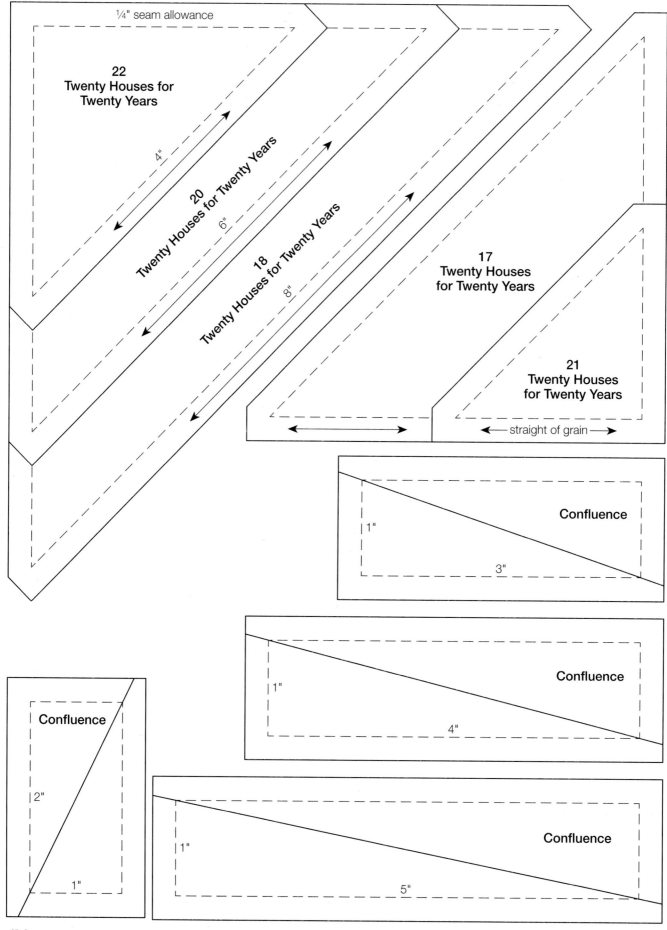

22
Twenty Houses for Twenty Years

4"

20
Twenty Houses for Twenty Years

6"

18
Twenty Houses for Twenty Years

8"

¼" seam allowance

17
Twenty Houses for Twenty Years

21
Twenty Houses for Twenty Years

← straight of grain →

Confluence

1"

3"

Confluence

1"

4"

Confluence

2"

1"

Confluence

1"

5"

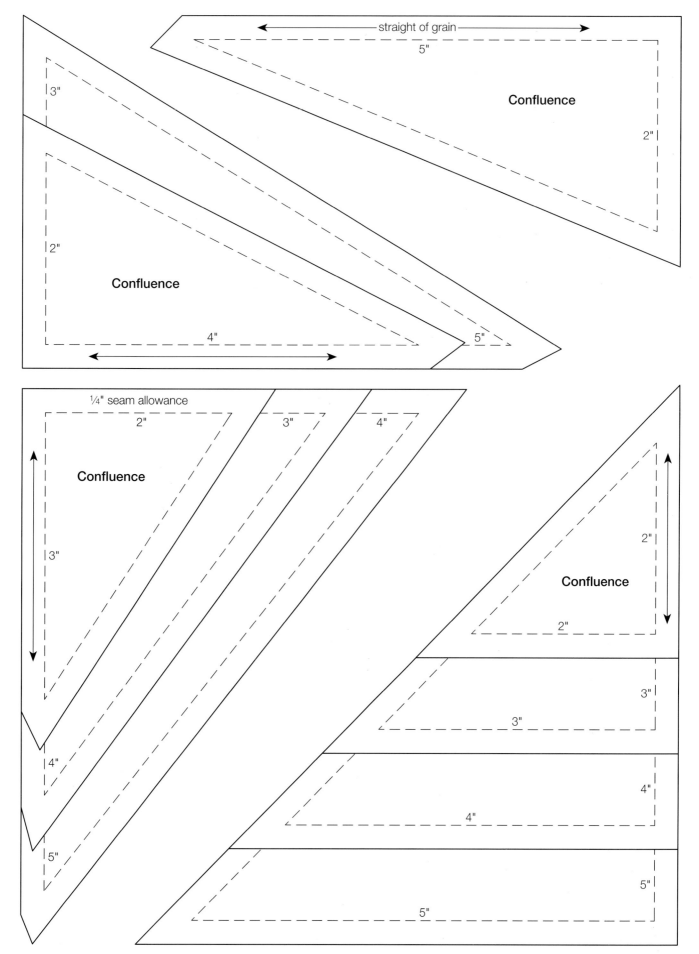

straight of grain

5"

Confluence

2"

3"

2"

Confluence

4"

5"

¼" seam allowance

2"

3"

4"

Confluence

3"

4"

5"

Confluence

2"

2"

3"

3"

4"

4"

5"

5"

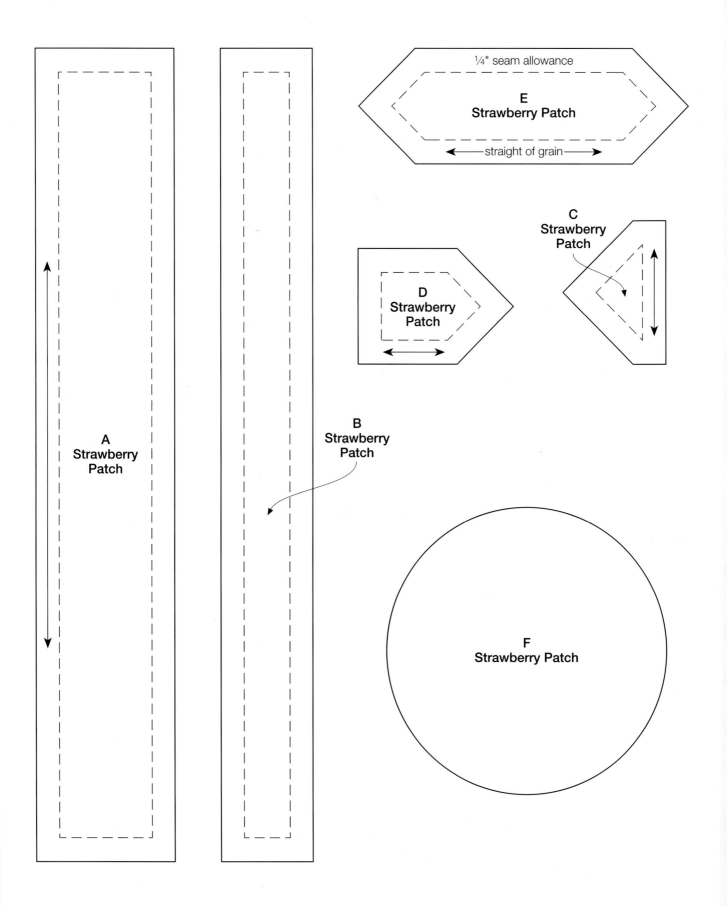

¼" seam allowance

E
Strawberry Patch

← straight of grain →

C
Strawberry
Patch

D
Strawberry
Patch

A
Strawberry
Patch

B
Strawberry
Patch

F
Strawberry Patch

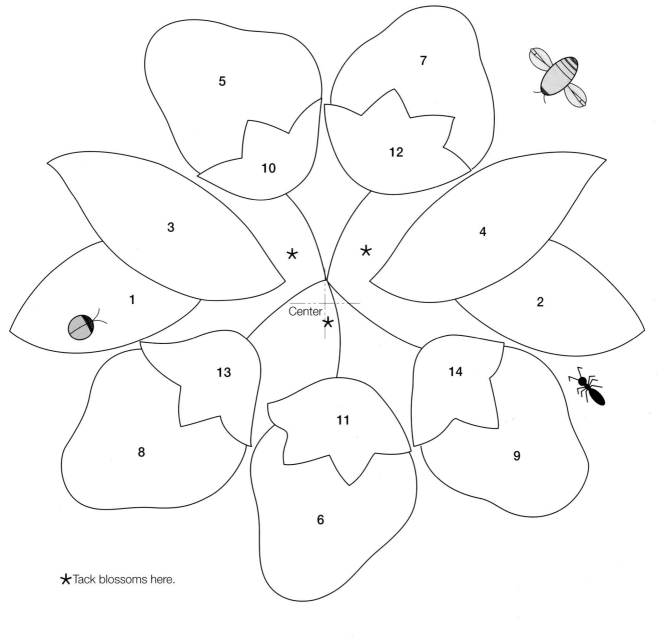

5

7

3

10

12

4

1

★

★

Center

★

2

13

14

8

11

9

6

★Tack blossoms here.

Strawberry Patch
Appliqué Pattern

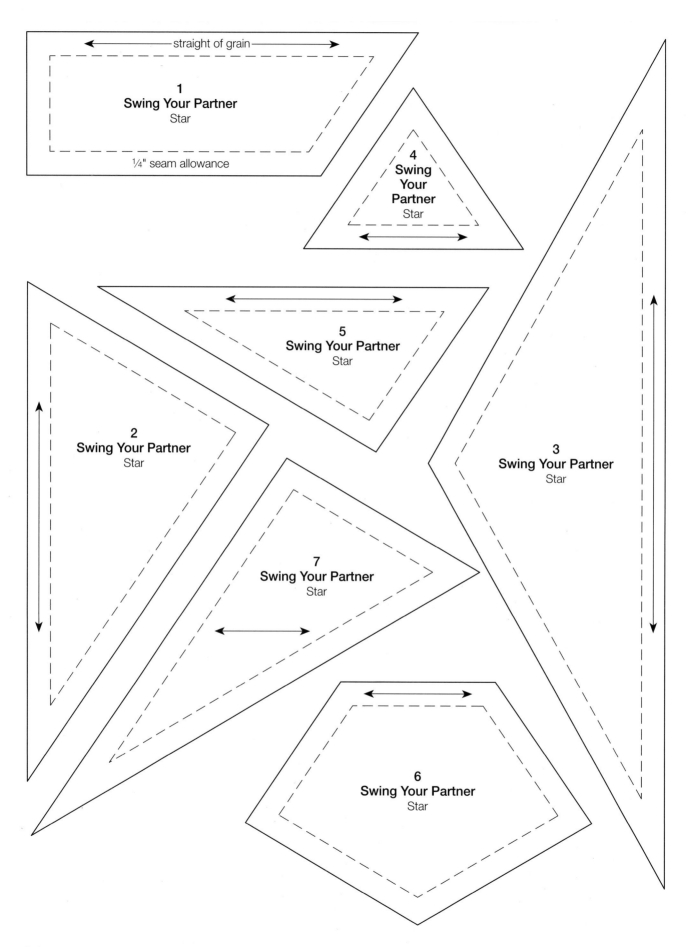

straight of grain

1
Swing Your Partner
Star

¼" seam allowance

4
**Swing
Your
Partner**
Star

5
Swing Your Partner
Star

2
Swing Your Partner
Star

3
Swing Your Partner
Star

7
Swing Your Partner
Star

6
Swing Your Partner
Star

Swing Your Partner
Horseshoe

Swing Your Partner
Goat

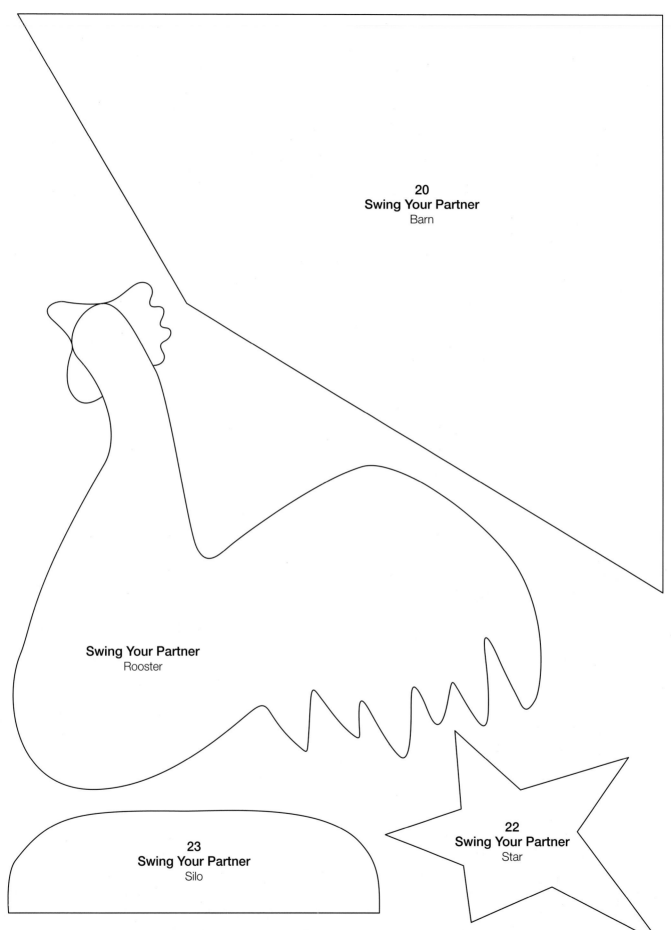

20
Swing Your Partner
Barn

Swing Your Partner
Rooster

23
Swing Your Partner
Silo

22
Swing Your Partner
Star

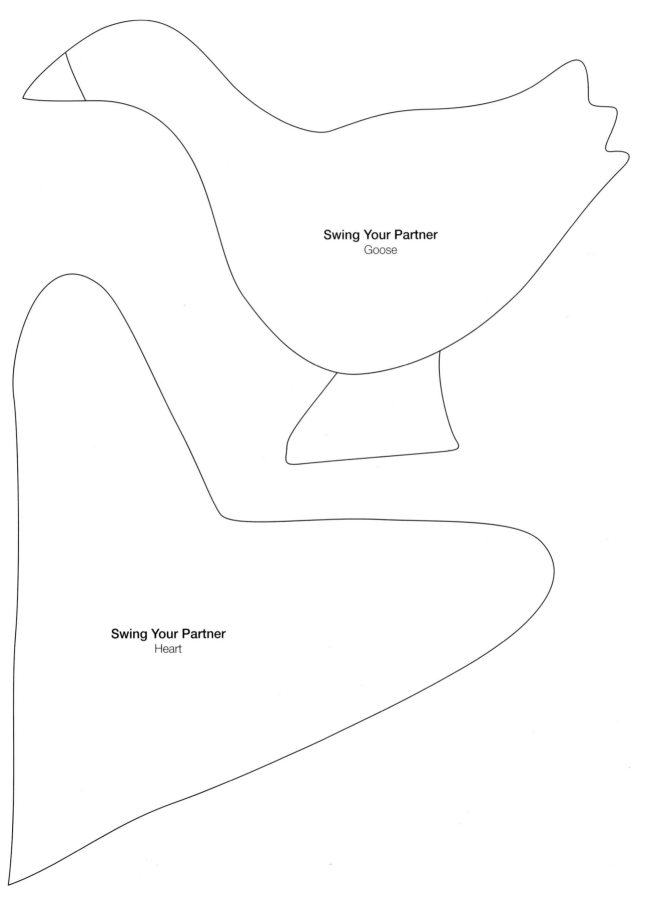

Swing Your Partner
Goose

Swing Your Partner
Heart

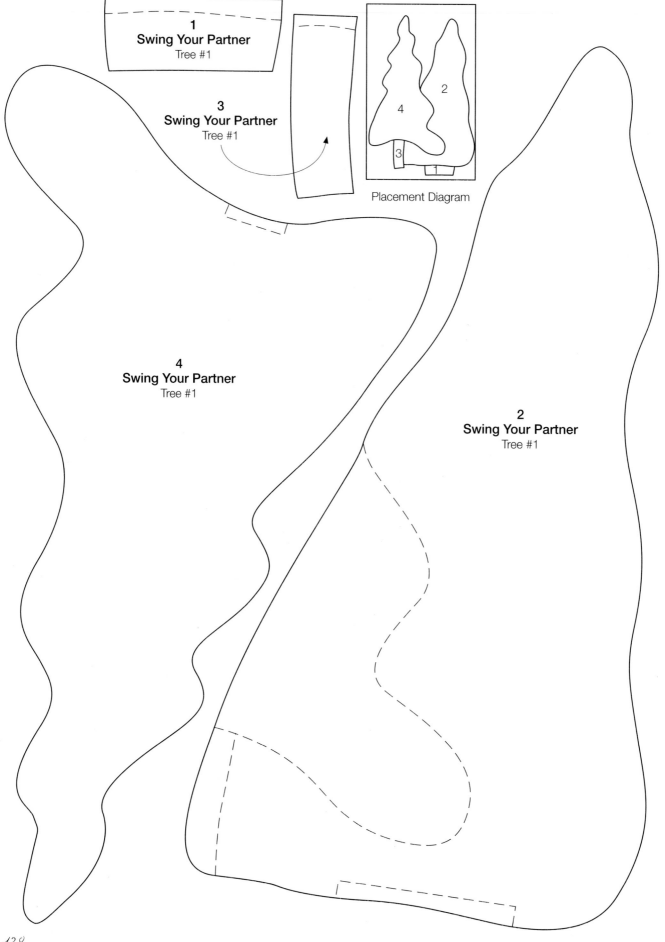

1
Swing Your Partner
Tree #1

3
Swing Your Partner
Tree #1

Placement Diagram

4
Swing Your Partner
Tree #1

2
Swing Your Partner
Tree #1

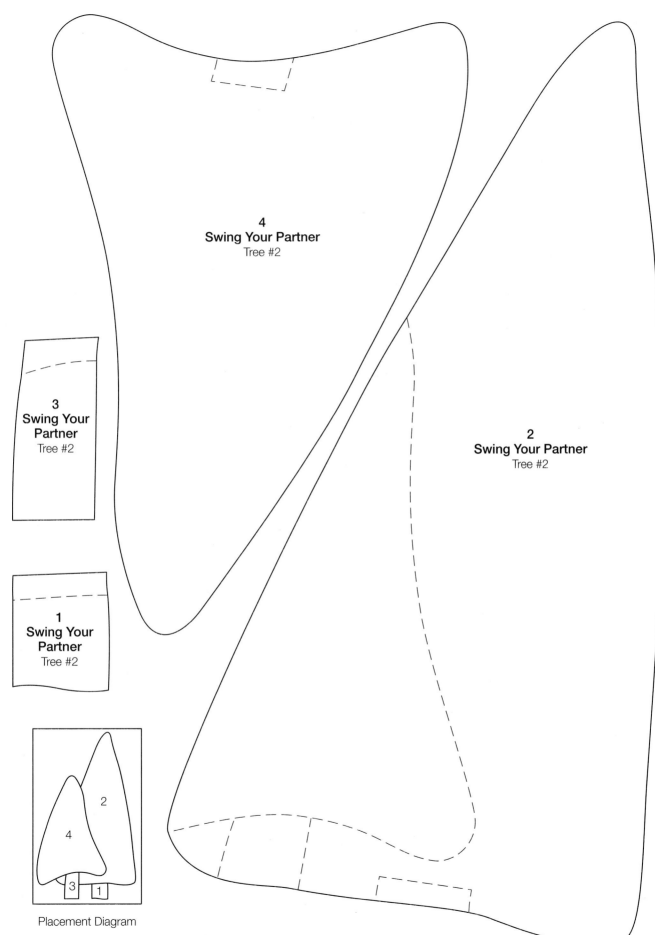

4
Swing Your Partner
Tree #2

3
Swing Your Partner
Tree #2

2
Swing Your Partner
Tree #2

1
Swing Your Partner
Tree #2

Placement Diagram

139

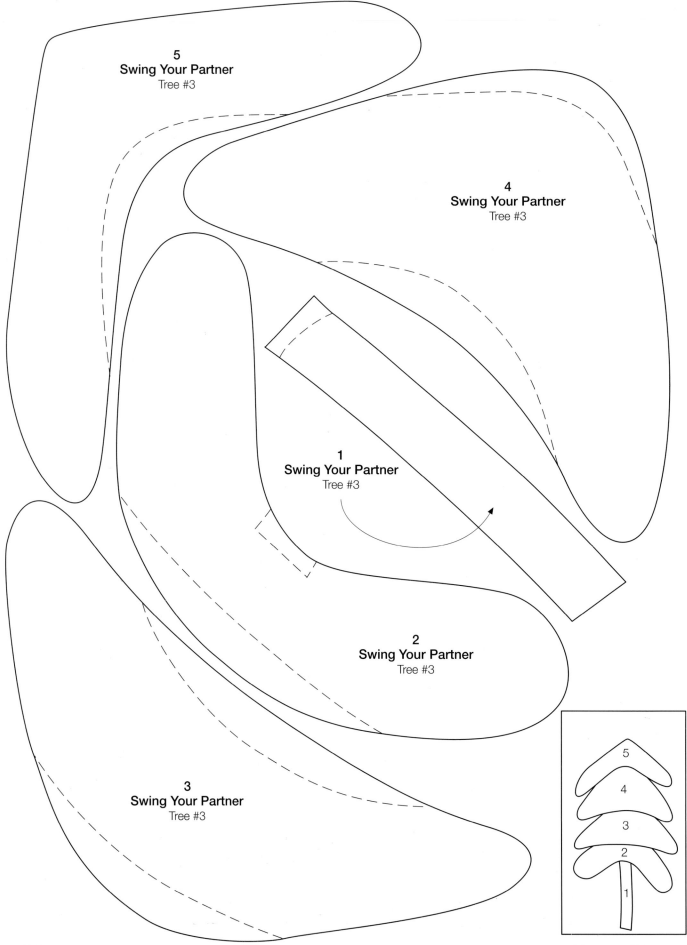

5
Swing Your Partner
Tree #3

4
Swing Your Partner
Tree #3

1
Swing Your Partner
Tree #3

2
Swing Your Partner
Tree #3

3
Swing Your Partner
Tree #3

Placement Diagram

Drink the Living Water
Appliqué Templates

Draw eyes and legs
with permanent ink pen.

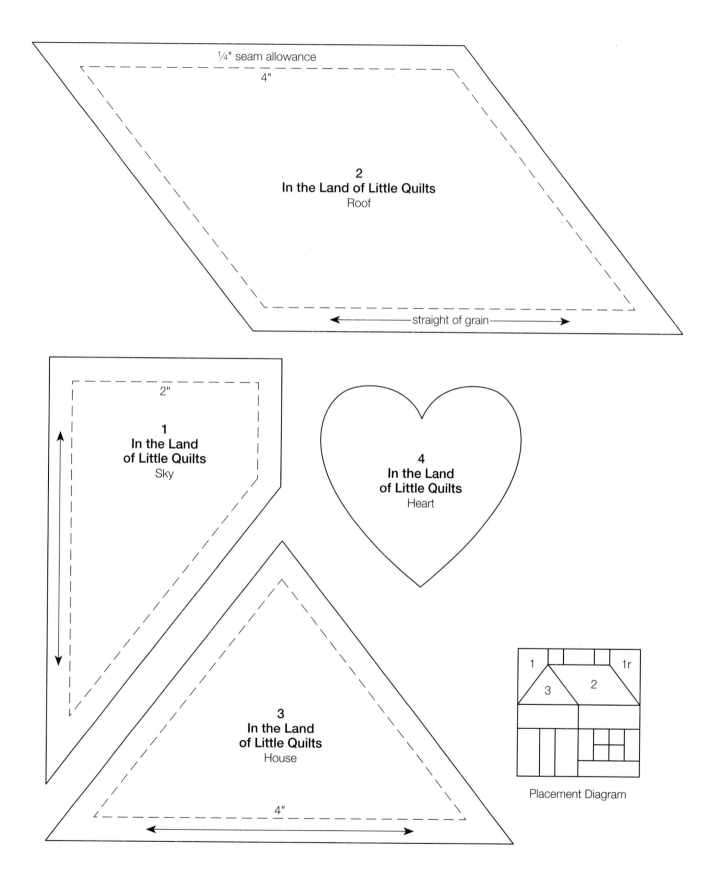

¼" seam allowance

4"

2
In the Land of Little Quilts
Roof

◄─────── straight of grain ───────►

2"

1
**In the Land
of Little Quilts**
Sky

4
**In the Land
of Little Quilts**
Heart

3
**In the Land
of Little Quilts**
House

4"

1   1r

3   2

Placement Diagram

Publications and Products

4", 6", 8" & metric Bias Square® • BiRangle™
Ruby Beholder® • ScrapMaster • Bias Stripper®
Shortcuts to America's Best-Loved Quilts (video)

Many titles are available at your local quilt shop.
For more information, write for a free color catalog
to That Patchwork Place, Inc., PO Box 118, Bothell,
WA 98041-0118 USA.

☎ U.S. and Canada, call **1-800-426-3126** for the
name and location of the quilt shop nearest you.
Int'l: 1-425-483-3313 **Fax:** 1-425-486-7596
E-mail: info@patchwork.com
Web: www.patchwork.com   8.97